GUITAR *signature licks*

BLUES ROCK
GUITAR MASTERS

MW00710920

Cover 'axe' provided by our friends at Fender Custom Shop

ISBN 0-634-00103-5

Visit Hal Leonard Online at **www.halleonard.com**

HAL•LEONARD®
CORPORATION

7777 W. BLUEMOUND RD. P.O. BOX 13819
MILWAUKEE, WISCONSIN 53213

TABLE OF CONTENTS

Page	Title	CD Track
4	Introduction	1
4	The Recording	
5	Acknowledgments	
	Tuning	2–3
6	**Badge**	4–7
13	**Strange Brew**	8–15
21	**Still Alive and Well**	16–21
26	**Rock and Roll Hoochie Koo**	22–26
32	**Statesboro Blues**	27–32
39	**Whipping Post**	33–39
47	**The Stumble**	40–44
52	**Someday, After Awhile**	45–49
56	**Hey Joe**	50–52
61	**Killing Floor**	53–58
66	**Lazy**	59–66
73	**Smoke on the Water**	67–71
78	**Rock My Plimsoul**	72–77
85	**Let Me Love You**	78–83
94	**Mississippi Queen**	84–87
99	**Dreams of Milk & Honey**	88–91
106	**Pride and Joy**	92–98

INTRODUCTION

Blues/Rock Guitar Masters Signature Licks offers detailed analysis and instruction on the playing of the greatest blues/rock guitarists that have ever lived. Never before have so many of these legendary guitarists been analyzed within the confines of a single book. The nine guitar heroes presented here are Jimi Hendrix, Eric Clapton, Stevie Ray Vaughan, Johnny Winter, Jeff Beck, Duane Allman, Richie Blackmore, Leslie West, and Peter Green.

Blues/Rock Guitar Masters examines the playing of each of these guitarists within the context of their greatest recordings, such as Jimi Hendrix's "Hey Joe," Stevie Ray Vaughan's "Pride and Joy," Leslie West's "Mississippi Queen," Jeff Beck's "Rock My Plimsoul," and Johnny Winter's "Still Alive and Well."

In this book, each of these classic songs has been segmented into the individual sections, such as intro, verse, pre-chorus, chorus, solo, bridge, and outro. Each song segment is presented with all of the guitar parts fully transcribed and recreated on the accompanying CD, as performed by a full band. All of the guitar solos are also performed slowly on the CD for easier understanding. Performance notes outlining chord voicings, scale use, unusual techniques, etc., are included in the text for each song.

On the accompanying CD, every attempt was made to recreate the sound of the original recordings in terms of guitar tone and panning. The overall intent is to present a mix that accentuates the guitar tracks more clearly than they appear on the original recordings, enabling one to focus on all of the subtle nuances of each performance. Each song excerpt begins with a four-beat countoff sounded by the hi-hat.

THE RECORDING

In an attempt to accurately recreate the guitar tones of the original recordings, I tried to use either the exact same type of guitar that appeared on those recordings, or a guitar that yielded a very similar and appropriate tone.

Eric Clapton is well known for using a wide variety of guitars, especially early in his career when he favored Gibsons. For "Badge," I used a '61 rosewood-board Fender Stratocaster for the rhythm parts (including the keyboard parts, which were arranged for and performed on guitar). This guitar part was actually performed by George Harrison of the Beatles, whose main guitar at the time was his custom-painted pre-CBS Strat. A beautiful, recently-issued Historic Gibson Les Paul was chosen for Eric's legendary solo. For "Strange Brew," a luscious '60 dot-neck Gibson ES335 delivered the goods.

Johnny Winter's "Still Alive and Well" called for a '64 Gibson Firebird V (this particular axe was given the nod of approval by Johnny Winter himself). For "Rock and Roll Hoochie Koo," Johnny's parts were performed on the Firebird, while Rick Derringer's hard-drivin' rhythm parts were performed on the Les Paul.

Duane Allman generally used a Gibson SG when he played slide guitar, but since none was available, I used a Gibson Melody Maker with a single humbucking pickup in the bridge position. For Dickey Betts' rhythm parts, the Les Paul was once again pressed into service. Both Duane and Dickey's guitar parts on "Whipping Post" were recorded with the Historic Les Paul, but a different one—one with a warmer, more "vintage" tone—was used for Duane's solos.

Peter Green may be best known as the composer of Santana's hit song, "Black Magic Woman," but he is also one of the most talented and influential guitarists in the history of blues-based rock. His introduction to the world at large occurred with the 1967 release of John Mayall and the Bluesbreakers' *A Hard Road* (London). At the time of this release, Green had just replaced the Cream-bound Eric Clapton in the Bluesbreakers—very large shoes to fill indeed. As evidenced by the two Green tracks included here, "The Stumble" and "Someday, After a While," Peter was certainly the right man for the job. Like

Eric, Green relied on a flametop Gibson Les Paul while in the Bluesbreakers, so a Les Paul was used to recreate his entries in this book.

Jimi Hendrix is the guitar player most closely associated with the Fender Stratocaster; because of Jimi, the Strat remains the most popular guitar today. On the two Hendrix songs included here, "Hey Joe" and "Killing Floor," the '61 Strat was used.

Another Stratocaster devotee is Deep Purple's Richie Blackmore. Richie prefers the maple fretboard variety, though, so a Fender Custom Shop relic with a maple board was used for the two Deep Purple songs, "Lazy" and "Smoke on the Water."

Jeff Beck, like Clapton, has used a wide variety of guitars throughout his career. At the time of his first recording as a leader, the incendiary *Truth* (Epic) album, his main axe was a flametop Les Paul. Yet another Gibson Custom Shop Historic Les Paul was used for both "Rock My Plimsoul" and "Let Me Love You."

Any list of rock's greatest guitarists would be incomplete without the incredible Leslie West. Leslie is best known for his work with the band Mountain, whose biggest hit is the rock-radio staple, "Mississippi Queen," included in this collection. Before the formation of Mountain, however, Leslie released a solo album called *Mountain*, an incredible disc that featured the very heavy track, "Dreams of Milk and Honey," which features one of the greatest guitar solos he ever recorded. (For this reason, this tune has been included here as well.) Leslie relied on a Les Paul Junior in those days, but as one was not available at the time of these recordings, a Les Paul Standard was used instead.

Stevie Ray Vaughan, like Jimi Hendrix, relied on Fender Stratocasters almost exclusively. The '61 was used for this recording of "Pride and Joy."

As devoted to vintage amplifiers as I may be, I opted to use a Line 6 POD to record all of the guitar and bass tracks on this CD. The unit is nothing short of amazing; it yielded beautifully accurate tones, achieved with a minimum amount of hair-pulling. From the sweet slide sound of Duane Allman, to the crushing distortion of Jimi Hendrix, to the laser-like clarity of Richie Blackmore, the POD proved that it was up to the task. It even worked very well for recording bass parts, using the Tube Pre-amp setting combined with compression.

Two basses were used for these recordings: a 1967 Gibson EB-2 and a 1986 ESP J-Bass, fitted with Seymour Duncan "Bass Lines" pickups. All bass tracks were transcribed from the original recordings and recreated note-for-note.

The drum tracks were all transcribed from the original recordings and meticulously programmed into an Alesis SR-16 drum machine.

All of the tracks were recorded onto a Tascam DA-88 digital eight-track, using a Mackie 1604 mixing console and mixed down to a Tascam DA-30 MK II DAT machine and a Phillips CDR 775 CD burner. Signal processing included Alesis Midiverb 4, Microverb III, and 3630 compressor.

ACKNOWLEDGMENTS

THANKS TO: Tracey, Rory, and Wyatt; Brad Tolinski and all at *Guitar World*; all at Hal Leonard Corporation; James Santiago and all at Line 6; Flip Scipio; Larry Fitzgerald; Dave Nesdall; Bill Bonanzinga; Vicky Hardy; John Ellis.

SPECIAL THANKS TO: Steve Lobmeier at D'Addario Strings; Evan Scopt at Seymour Duncan Pickups; Bill Mohroff at TEAC; Mitch Colby at Marshall/Korg; Richie Fliegler at Fender USA; Gary Blankenburg at Music Services; and of course, Ed Cavaseno for drumming on "Hey Joe," and Paul Apostilides and Richard Rosch for providing the human rhythm section on "The Stumble" and "Someday After a While" (also available on my first CD, *Put a Sock in It*).

Any questions? Visit the website www.andyaledort.com, or send an email to: aaledort@ix.netcom.com.

ERIC CLAPTON: with Cream

BADGE
From the Cream album *Goodbye* (Polydor)
Words and Music by Eric Clapton and George Harrison

By any account, Eric Clapton is one of the most important and influential blues/rock guitarists that ever lived. Based on the fact that his playing had a marked impact on such luminaries as Jimi Hendrix, Jimmy Page, Jeff Beck, Peter Green, Duane Allman, Leslie West, Mick Taylor, Johnny Winter, and Mike Bloomfield, among many others, he may very well be the most important blues/rock guitarist that has ever lived. His stint with bassist Jack Bruce and drummer Ginger Baker in Cream set the template for heavy blues-based rock while coining the term "power trio." His magical, inspired playing from this era continues to influence guitarists the world over.

In October of '68, scarcely a month after Eric Clapton lent brilliant guitar work to George Harrison's Beatles *White Album* track, "While My Guitar Gently Weeps," George returned the favor by co-writing and recording this Cream song with Eric. George is credited as "L'Angelo Misterioso, rhythm guitar," and the popular misconception was that he played the heavily-Leslied arpeggiated bridge lick. In truth, George played all of the rhythm guitar tracks until that point, and the bridge rhythm part and solo were played by Clapton.

Figure 1–Intro & First Verse

The "Badge" intro features one primary rhythm guitar part, notated below as Gtr. 1. This part, treated with moderately fast amp tremolo, is based on the alternating of two fifth-position barre chords, Am7 and D. On beats 2 and 4, dead-string accents are performed to strengthen the "backbeat" feel of the song. In fact, there is a second guitar, shown as Gtr. 2 and written in slashes above the Gtr. 1 part, which strikes muted string accents on all four downbeats of each measure.

At the first verse, the chord progression is introduced: Am–D–Em (two times) C–Am–Bm–Am9. On the Em chord in measures 7 and 11, notice that Esus2 is played briefly in the first half of each measure. In this arrangement, producer Felix Pappalardi's piano part has been arranged for guitar; this part makes use of high chord voicings that complement the primary rhythm guitar part well.

Featured Guitar:
Gtr. 1 meas. 1-17

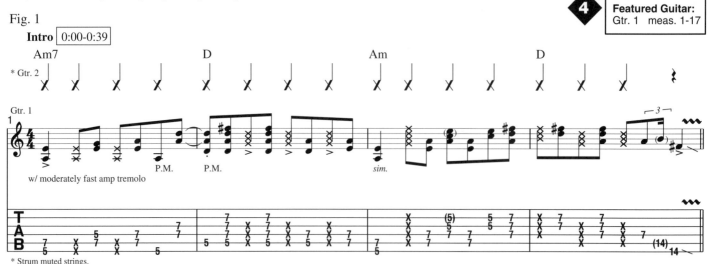

Fig. 1
Intro 0:00-0:39

* Strum muted strings.

First Verse

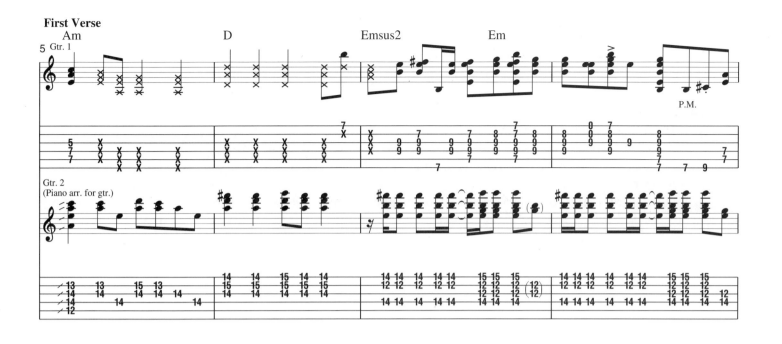

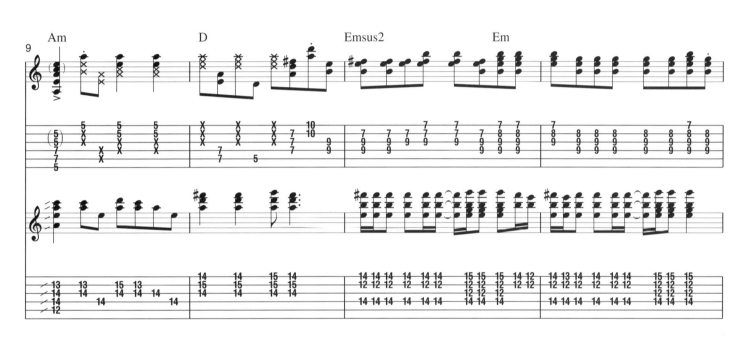

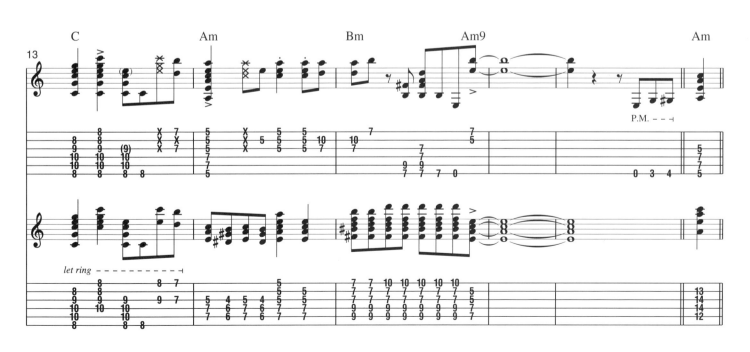

Figure 2–Bridge (with four-measure pickup)

It is at this point that Eric first begins playing on the track. The primary chord progression of D–Cmaj7–G/B–G, performed by Gtr. 1, is arpeggiated throughout, with all notes allowed to ring as long as possible. Begin by picking the open D string, followed by F♯ fretted with the ring finger and A fretted with the index finger. Then bring the middle finger down on the third fret of the A string to initiate the arpeggiation of Cmaj7.

Gtr. 2 enters in the last measure of the four-measure pickup on the upbeat of beat four, and supplies full-voiced major chord accents throughout. Notice that all of the sixth-string root notes for these chord voicings are fretted with the thumb. Gtr. 1 continues the arpeggiated rhythm part, and both guitars maintain their respective parts through the subsequent guitar solo.

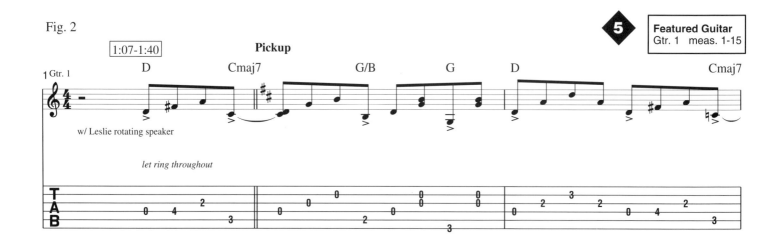

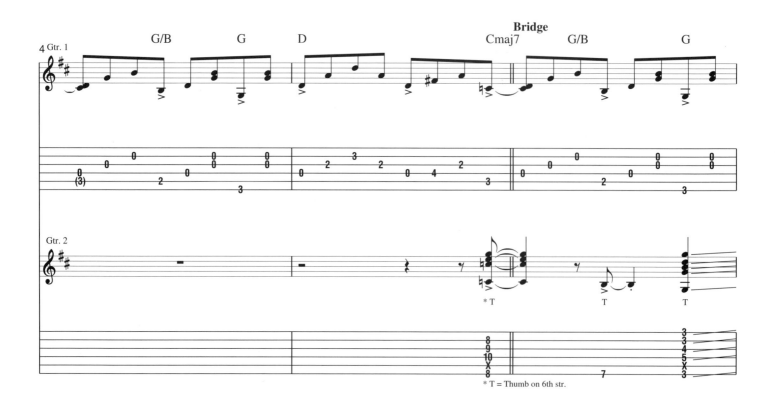

* T = Thumb on 6th str.

Figure 3–Solo

Over the rhythm guitar parts introduced at the bridge, Eric Clapton plays one of his greatest guitar solos. This solo has it all. It is insistently and undeniably melodic, it's phrased and articulated to absolute perfection, and the tone—sounds like either a Gibson 335 or a Firebird I—is beautiful. At the grand old age of twenty-three, Eric was living up to the "Clapton Is God" graffiti that adorned the streets of London at that time.

This solo is based primarily on D minor pentatonic (D–F–G–A–C), with brief allusions to the D Mixolydian mode (D–E–F♯–G–A–B–C) via the inclusion of the major 3rd, F♯. Right from the start, Eric's string-bending intonation is impeccable: he begins with a "ghost bend" (also known as a "pre-bend") by bending C (string 2/fret 13) up one whole step to D before striking it, and then releases the bend one half step, sounding C♯. Eric uses the "ghost bend" technique liberally throughout this solo; another good example is found in measure 4, where F (string 1/fret 13) is bent up one half step to F♯.

In measures 4–6, Eric switches to D major pentatonic (D–E–F♯–A–B) before returning to D minor pentatonic at the end of measure 6 and into measures 7 and 8; he then returns to D major pentatonic in measures 9–11. In measures 12 and 13, he seamlessly works back into the "minor-3rd" sound of D minor pentatonic and wraps the solo up in measure 14 by starting with D major pentatonic and finishing with D minor pentatonic, as the song shifts back into the verse section. A purely exquisite rock guitar solo if there ever was one!

6 Featured Guitar:
Gtr. 3   meas. 1-16

7 Slow Demo:
Gtr. 3   meas. 1-16

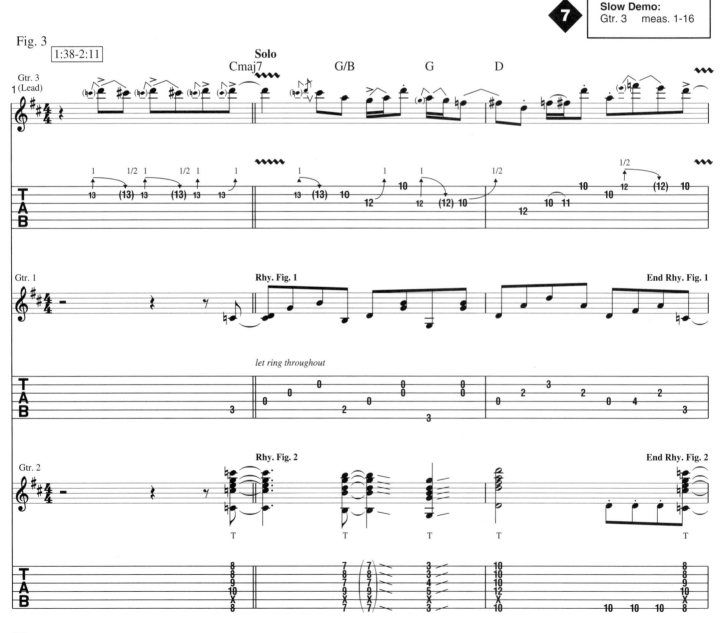

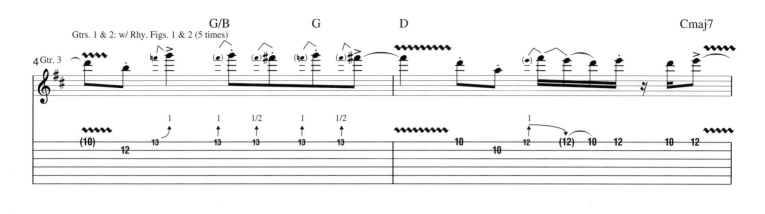

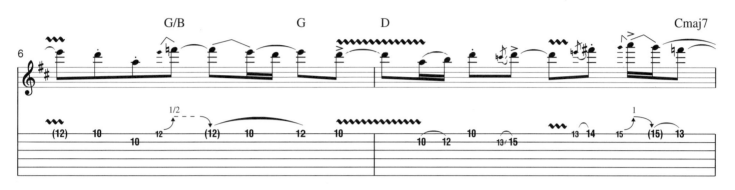

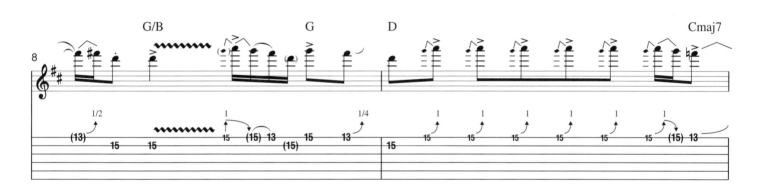

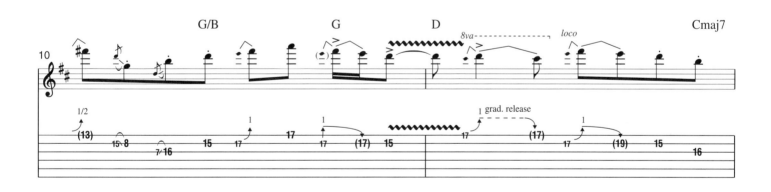

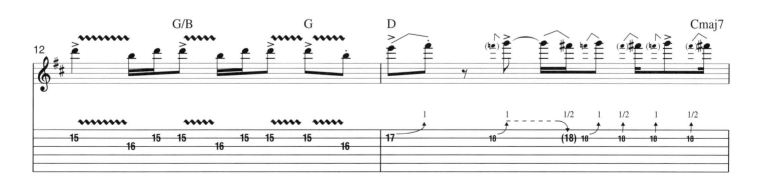

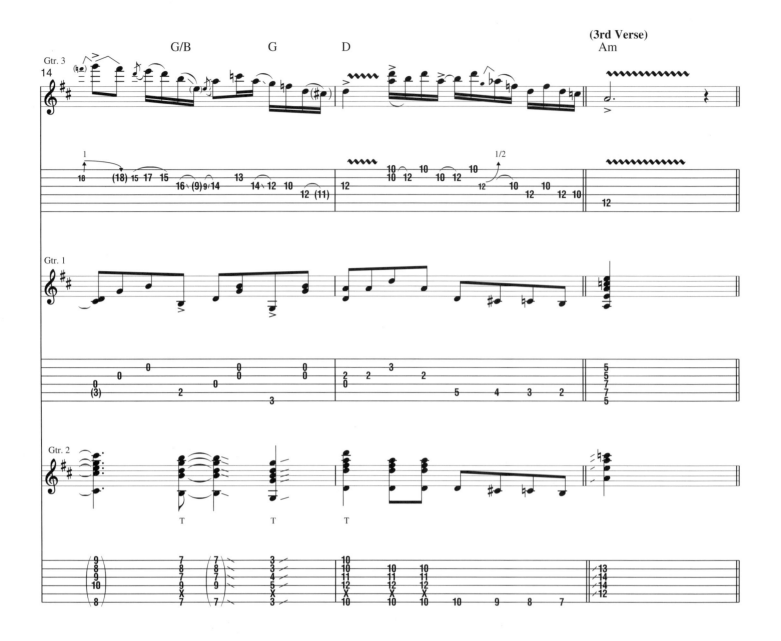

STRANGE BREW
from *Disraeli Gears* (Polydor)
Words and Music by Eric Clapton, Felix Pappalardi and Gail Collins

"Strange Brew," one of the big hits from Cream's second LP *Disraeli Gears*, is actually a retooling of the blues classic, "Hey, Lawdy Mama." Looking for a vehicle for Eric as a vocalist, producer Felix Pappalardi took the "Hey, Lawdy Mama" backing track and created "Strange Brew." This turn of events was to the consternation of bassist Jack Bruce, because superimposing the "Strange Brew" structure over the existing backing track caused Jack's bass line to sound momentarily incorrect (in measure 2). Nevertheless, "Strange Brew" went on to become a huge hit and a time-honored Cream track.

Figure 4–Intro

This song features two guitar parts—one lead and one rhythm—throughout, both played by Clapton. The lead guitar (Gtr. 1) plays improvised solo figures based on A minor pentatonic (A–C–D–E–G), with the inclusion of the major 3rd (C♯) usually bent up from C. Eric's solo lines are very melodic; the riff across measures 1 and 2 recalls the intro figures heard on blues harmonica great Little Walter's "Everything's Going to Be Alright." The tone is simply glorious. The rhythm guitar (Gtr. 2) combines chordal stabs with single-note, bass line-like figures also based on A minor pentatonic.

"Strange Brew" is a 12-bar blues, but the intro is slightly different from the rest of the song. During the intro, the I chord (A) is held for the first four measures; during the rest of the song, the first four measures of the progression consist of one measure of A followed by one measure of the IV chord (D) and then two measures of A. Switching to the IV chord in measure 2 of a 12-bar blues is commonly referred to as a "quick IV."

8   **Featured Guitar:**
Gtr. 1   meas. 1-12

9   **Slow Demo:**
Gtr. 1   meas. 1-12

Fig. 4

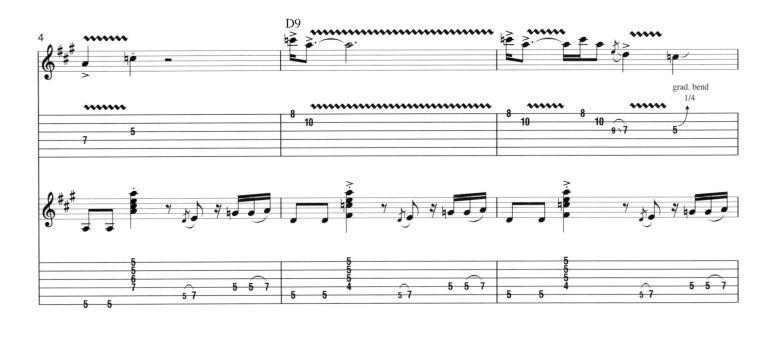

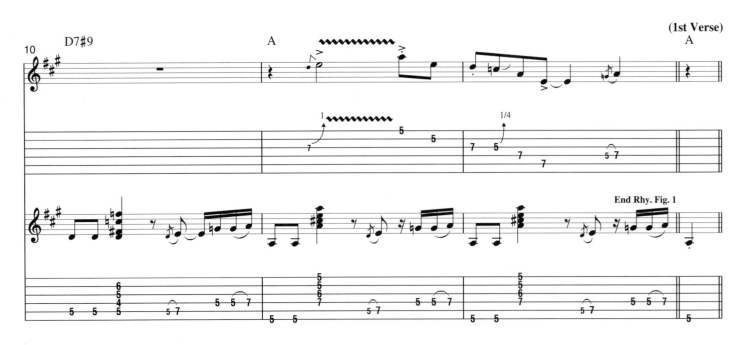

Figure 5–First Verse

The Gtr. 2 rhythm part is identical to that played during the intro, save for the "quick IV" as previously mentioned. The lead guitar *obbligato* figures are sparse as they serve to "answer" the vocal phrases. Eric's solo figures are again based on A minor pentatonic. Though many of the licks Eric plays on this song seem to point to the influence of Albert King, Eric himself has stated that his playing here is more indebted to Buddy Guy.

Figure 6–Second Verse

The same principles apply to the second verse as the first, with the rhythm guitar part complemented by solo phrases (still based on A minor pentatonic) in the spaces left by the vocal. The last measure of this section serves as the pickup measure for the solo, which begins with a very wide, two-step bend (à la Albert King). There is one subtle difference in the rhythm guitar part, as D9 is played in measure 10 instead of the previously used D7#9.

11   **Full Band**

Fig. 6
Second Verse [0:55-1:22]

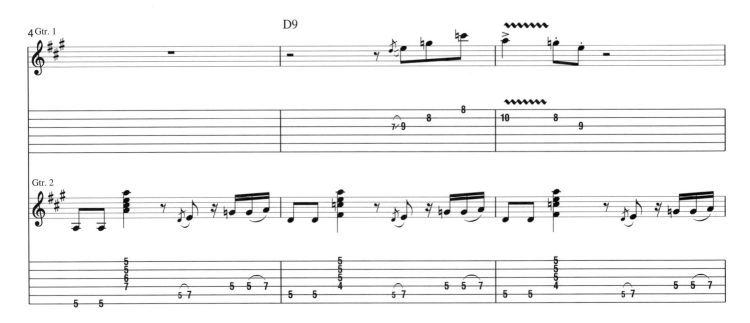

Figure 7–Solo

Eric begins this solo with a huge, Albert King-style two-step bend, as a fretted D (string 2/fret 15) is pushed all the way up to sound a high G. This entire solo is based on A minor pentatonic with the subtle inclusion of the major third (C#). In measure 2, the bend from D to E on beat 2 sounds slightly sharp, which was most likely unintentional. The solo as a whole features slow and deliberate lines performed with authority and grace. The solo concludes in measure 12 with an E/C# double-stop, with the C# hammered on from C natural one half step below. This is a signature technique employed by Eric on a few other occasions, such as the intro to Eric's recording of "All Your Love" while a member of John Mayall's Bluesbreakers (check out *Eric Clapton: The Bluesman Signature Licks* for a detailed analysis).

During this solo, the rhythm guitar part remains virtually identical to what is played during the verse sections.

12 Featured Guitar:
Gtr. 1 meas. 1-12

13 Slow Demos:
Gtr. 1 meas. 1-12

Fig. 7

Solo 1:22-1:49

Gtr. 2: w/ Rhy. Fig. 1

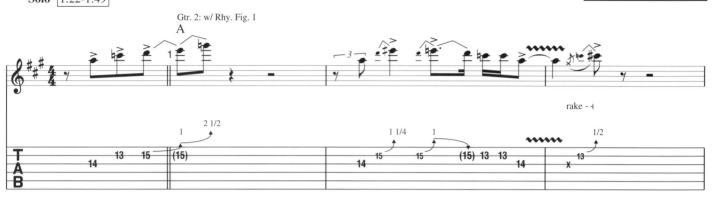

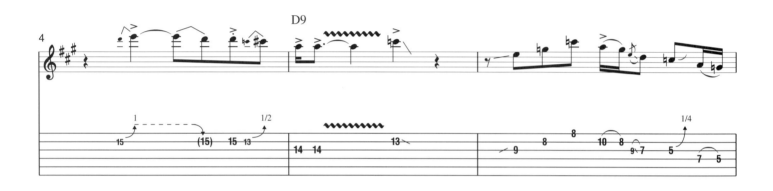

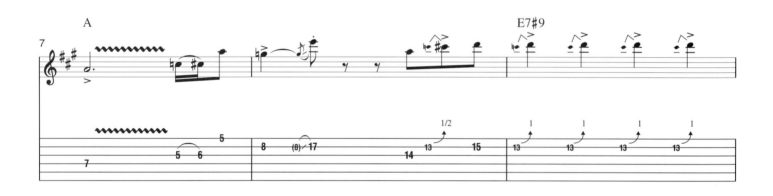

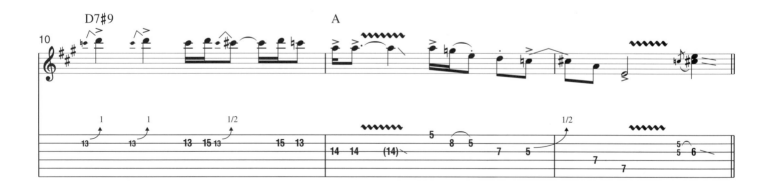

Figure 8–Outro

The "Strange Brew" outro follows the same arrangement concept as that of the verses, as the same basic rhythm part is abutted with vocal and lead guitar "trades." As before, Eric's lead lines are based on A minor pentatonic.

The song ends with a two-measure "band *tacet*," meaning that the band stops playing while the lead guitar plays a cadenza-like fill to end the song. This expressive two-measure phrase is not performed with pristine execution, and therein lies its charm. There is a bit of a lazy, off-balance feeling to the way Eric delivers this phrase, lending a unique sense of musicality. Lastly, the final A9 chord sounds unusual because bassist Jack Bruce plays a G note instead of A, placing the ♭7 as the chord's implied root note.

14 Featured Guitar:
Gtr. 1   meas. 1-12

15 Slow Demo:
Gtr. 1   meas. 1-12

Fig. 8
Outro   2:18-2:46

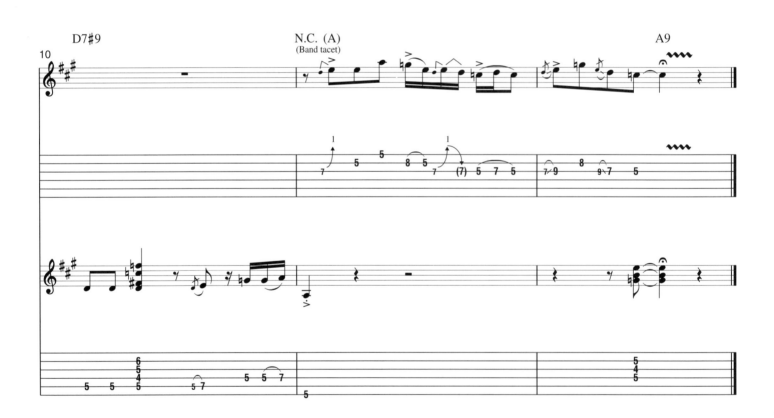

JOHNNY WINTER

STILL ALIVE AND WELL
From *Still Alive and Well* (Columbia)
Words and Music by Rick Derringer

If any guitarist from the '60s deserves to be placed shoulder to shoulder with the likes of Jimi Hendrix, Eric Clapton, and Jeff Beck, it's Johnny Winter. Possessing blazing speed, razor-sharp articulation, and an endless flow of brilliant ideas, Johnny Winter put more pure *blues* into the blues/rock genre than any of his highly touted contemporaries. Whether playing acoustic and electric slide or standard electric guitar, no one burns as white-hot as Beaumont, Texas's own Johnny Winter.

"Still Alive and Well" is the title track from Johnny's seminal "comeback" album of 1973 and offers indisputable evidence of the scope of his greatness and individuality. Written by legendary rock guitarist Rick Derringer, this song is the perfect vehicle for Johnny to showcase his formidable vocal and guitaristic abilities, as it is replete with solo bursts and hard-drivin' rhythm parts. And let's not forget his classic spoken intro, "I'm hungry—let's do this f***er!"

Figure 9–Intro and First Verse

The "Still Alive and Well" intro gets off to a rollicking start with a highly aggressive two-measure blast of molten blues/rock improvisation. Following the open A string pedal tone, Johnny plays a D-type "cowboy" chord up in twelfth position, which sounds Am7. (The chord name shown, A7#9, refers to the overall inherent harmony implied during the intro.) The subsequent single-note lines are based on A minor pentatonic (A–C–D–E–G). Across beats 3 and 4 of measure 2, the syncopated G–C, D–G single-note lick is played as a band figure and telegraphs the verse section's primary riff.

For the first four measures of the verse, Johnny plays a two-measure figure based on A minor pentatonic that utilizes the previous syncopated band figure. Measures 7–10 move through single measures of E7#9, F#m (with improvised F# minor pentatonic [F#–A–B–C#–E] licks thrown in), and G5, ending with D5 and E5 in the final measure. Johnny's attack throughout is very aggressive and *rock 'n' roll*; he was at the peak of his powers in those days, and, even within the confines of a recording studio, played with the same intensity as if he were performing in a packed stadium.

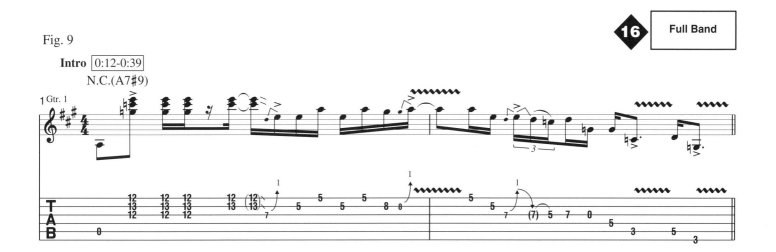

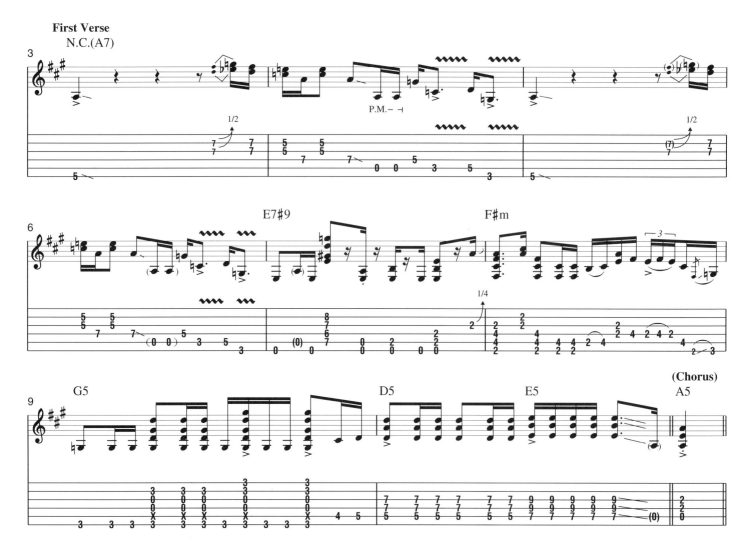

Figure 10–Chorus

The chorus consists of a blues-like I–IV–V chord progression of A–D–E, followed by a syncopated D5–C5–A chord movement. Johnny finishes off each of the two four-measure phrases with single-note improvisation: in measure 4, the "soloing" licks are based on A minor pentatonic; in measure 8, the licks are based on A major pentatonic (A–B–C#–E–F#). In measures 5–7, Johnny plays a very cool "funky blues" rhythm figure based on dominant seventh chords.

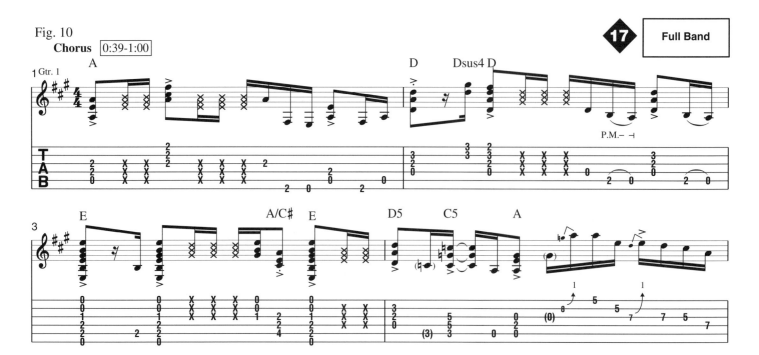

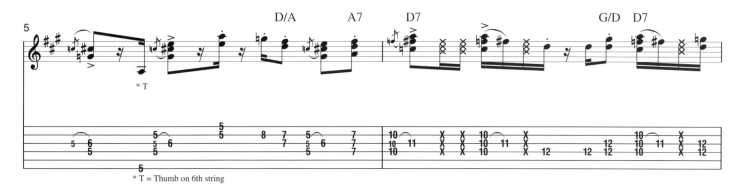

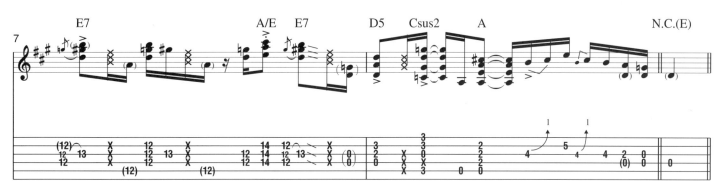

* T = Thumb on 6th string

Figure 11–Verse Tag (Solo)

Each verse section concludes with a brief four-measure workout over the V chord (E7). Johnny's beautifully fluid lines are based, in measures 1 and 2, on E minor pentatonic (E–G–A–B–D). Points of interest are: measure 1, last sixteenth note—B (string 2/fret 12) is bent up one whole step with the index finger and released; and measure 2, beat four—A (string 3/fret 14) is bent up one whole step to B and is held while a high E (string 1/fret 12) followed by D (string 2/fret 15) are "reverse raked" into the previously bent A-to-B. This "reverse rake" is performed by dragging the pick across the top three strings, starting from the highest string.

In measures 3 and 4, Johnny switches to lines based on E major pentatonic (E–F♯–G♯–B–C♯). Notice that all of the lines are phrased to perfection and delivered with great authority and conviction.

18   **Featured Guitar:** Gtr. 1   meas. 1-4

19   **Slow Demo:** Gtr. 1   meas. 1-4

Fig. 11

Verse Tag (Solo) [1:00-1:10]

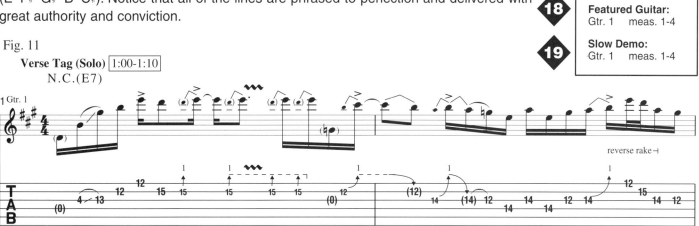

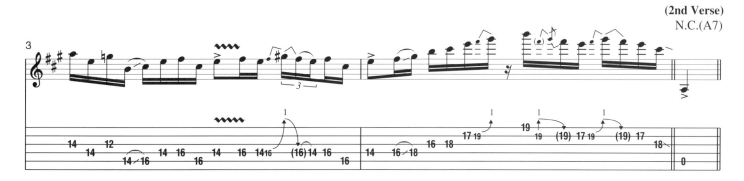

Figure 12–Solo

The solo section combines the chord progressions found on the verse and chorus sections, beginning with eight measures that replicate the first four measures of the verse section, played twice. Measures 9–16 are basically identical to the chorus progression.

For the first eight measures, Johnny relies on A minor pentatonic, ending each one-measure phrase with the verse section's signature band figure. The fast, ascending sixteenth-note triplet lick in measure 5 is a rock 'n' roll staple, employed to great effect by other rock guitarists such as Jimi Hendrix (on "Bold as Love") and Jimmy Page (on "Good Times, Bad Times") but played in reverse.

In measure 9, Johnny plays a very unusual *unison bend* lick. A unison bend is sounded when two strings are struck simultaneously, one of which is fretted normally while the other is bent to sound the same pitch as the fretted note. Johnny uses this technique here in conjunction with an unusual "three-on-four" syncopation, as a lick which is three sixteenth notes in length is played repeatedly across groups of four sixteenth notes.

Measure 10 features a rhythm guitar-like fill over D, based on sliding pairs of 6ths (beat 2), and measure 11, over E, is based on E minor pentatonic, followed by a return to A minor pentatonic in measure 12. In measure 13, Johnny shifts to the octave A minor pentatonic shape in seventeenth position and again uses the reverse rake technique on beat 3. After a brief reference to D minor pentatonic (D–F–G–A–C) in measure 14, he switches to E major pentatonic over E in measure 15, quickly moving back into A minor pentatonic across the last two beats of this measure and into measure 16. Master this solo and you'll be well on your way to "guitar god" status!

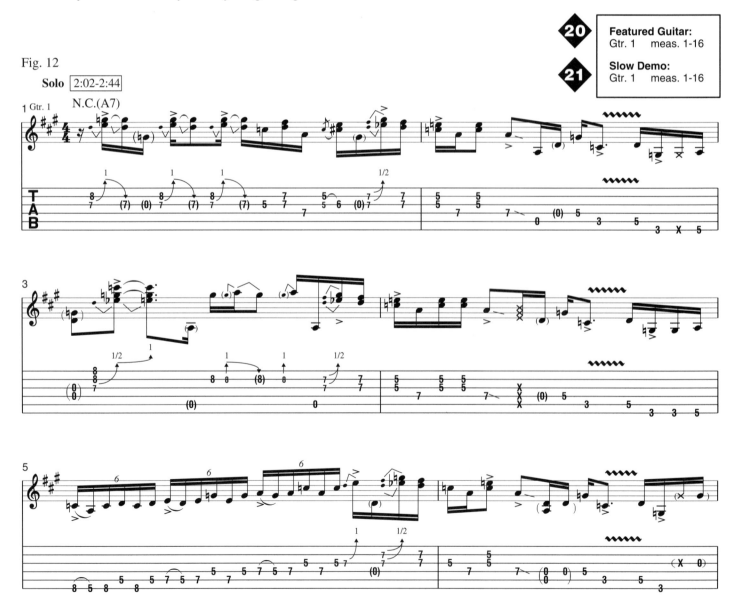

20 Featured Guitar:
Gtr. 1   meas. 1-16

21 Slow Demo:
Gtr. 1   meas. 1-16

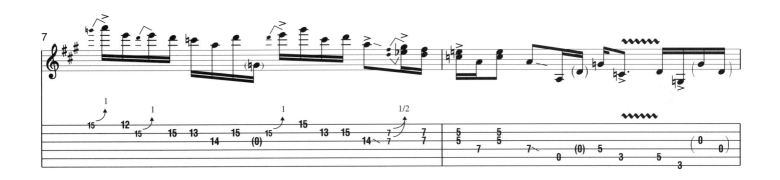

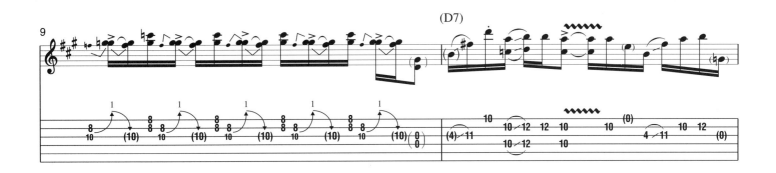

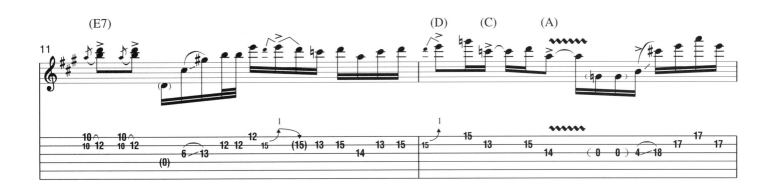

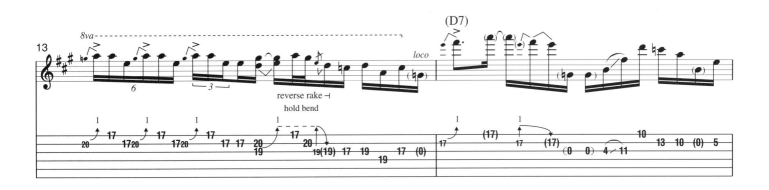

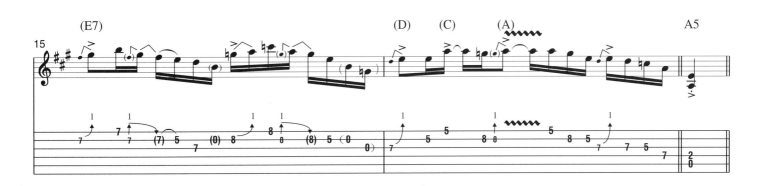

ROCK AND ROLL HOOCHIE KOO
From *Johnny Winter And* (Columbia)
Words and Music by Rick Derringer

Rick Derringer's version of "Rock and Roll Hoochie Koo," from his album *All American Boy*, is one of the most well-known classic rock songs of all time. But this earlier version, cut by Johnny Winter And, is, to my mind, far superior. As a band, Johnny Winter And had a distinctive, funky feel, fueled by the dual guitar prowess of Johnny and Rick. The Allman Brothers band is well-loved for the interplay between Duane Allman and Dickey Betts, but Johnny and Rick displayed an amazing chemistry that was every bit as impressive.

Figure 13–Intro

"Rock and Roll Hoochie Koo" features two distinct guitar parts throughout: Rick Derringer supplies the rock-solid rhythm work while Johnny Winter adds complementary chord voicings and improvised single-note lines. The intro to this song is in fact the same as the chorus. Johnny's part begins with unusual voicings on the top three strings for the F, B♭/F, G, and C/G chords, followed by a brief lead line based on the A blues scale (A–C–D–E♭–E–G). The majority of the improvisation in this song is based on this scale. Rick plays low-voiced power chords and major chords and displays a locked-in sense of time that has earned him respect as one of greatest rhythm guitarists ever. In measure four, Rick strums muted strings, accenting the first two sixteenth notes of beats 2 and 3.

Across the last two measures of the intro, Johnny and Rick play harmonized syncopated licks that make reference to the V chord, E7.

Full Band

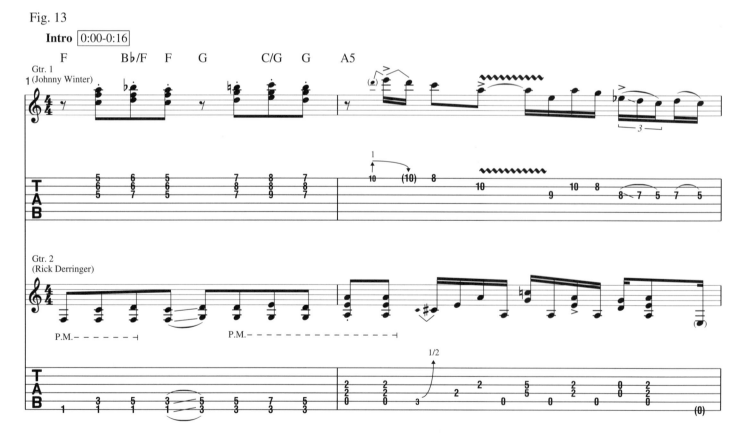

Fig. 13

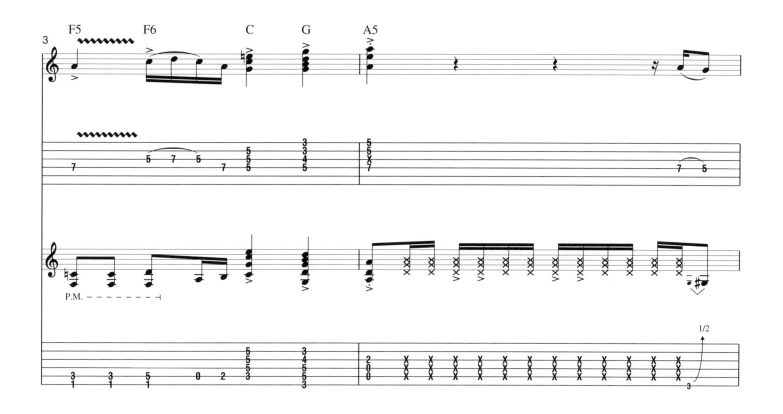

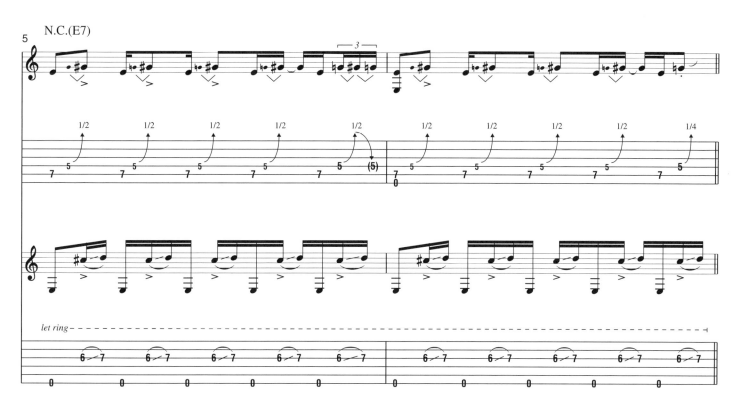

Figure 14–First Verse

Throughout the verse section, both Johnny and Rick add muted-string accents to their respective rhythm guitar parts; learn both parts and compare them to see how they lock in with each other. For both guitarists, the rhythm part consists of a power chord-driven progression of A5–C5–D5–C5.

In measures 2, 4, 6, and 8, the two guitarists play the same single-note melody doubled and harmonized in different registers: in measures 2 and 6, the melody is played an octave apart, with Johnny taking the high octave; in measures 4 and 8, Johnny harmonizes Rick's line a major 3rd above.

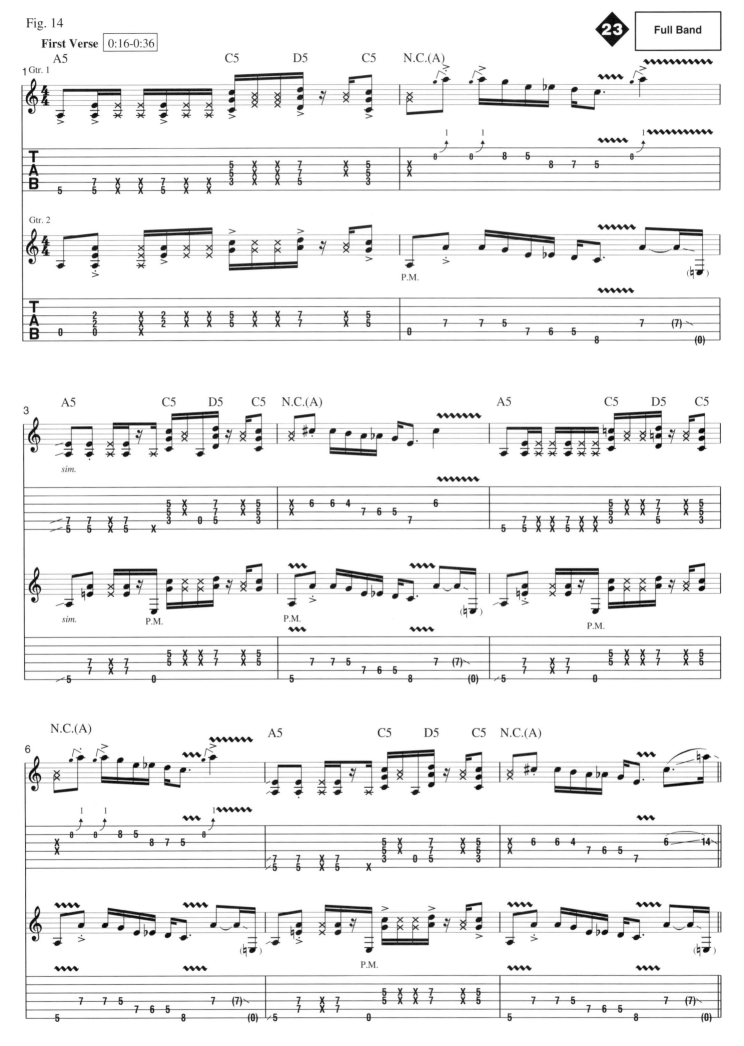

Figure 15–Chorus

As stated, the chorus is a restatement of the figures first presented in the intro, with Johnny performing high chord voicings and solo lines over Rick's driving rhythm part. Notice that Johnny's improvised lines, based still on A minor pentatonic, are slightly different than those played during the intro; of note is his lick in measure 4, which doubles Rick's rhythm guitar part one octave higher.

Fig. 15

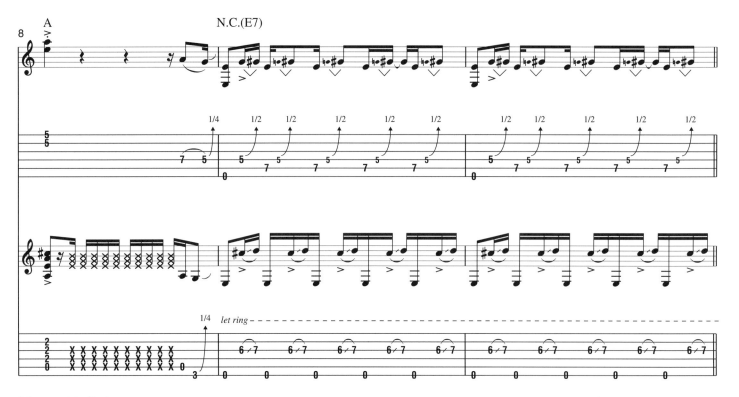

Figure 16–Solo

Johnny Winter's solo on this song is spectacular. The drive with which he phrases is relentless, as each knuckle-busting riff flows seamlessly into the next. Though the solo overflows with attitude and flash, its complex musicality should not be overlooked.

For the first three and a half measures, the solo is based on A minor pentatonic, shifting to A major pentatonic (A–B–C♯–E–F♯) in the second half of measure 4 and into measure 5. Measure 6 features a quick reference to D minor pentatonic (D–F–G–A–C), followed by a return to A minor pentatonic and the A blues scale (A–C–D–E♭–E–G) for the remainder of the solo. Johnny's articulation during this solo is crystal clear—listen to the abundance of razor-sharp pull-offs, such as those played in the last measure—and sets a standard for all guitarists to aspire to.

25 Featured Guitar:
Gtr. 1   meas. 1-8

26 Slow Demos:
Gtr. 1   meas. 1-8

Fig. 16

Solo | 1:47-2:07 |

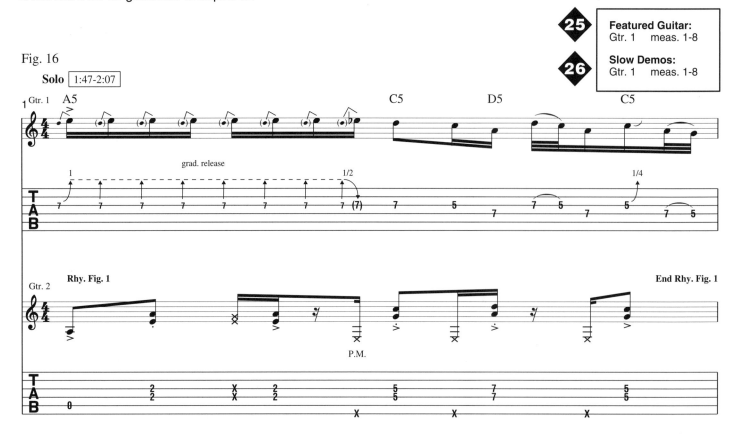

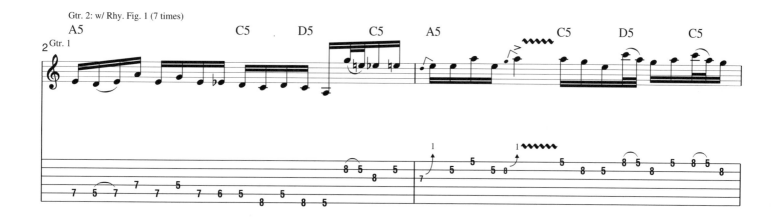

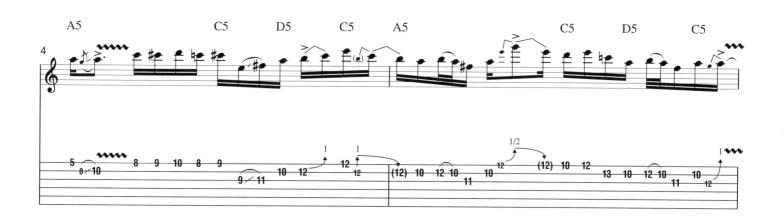

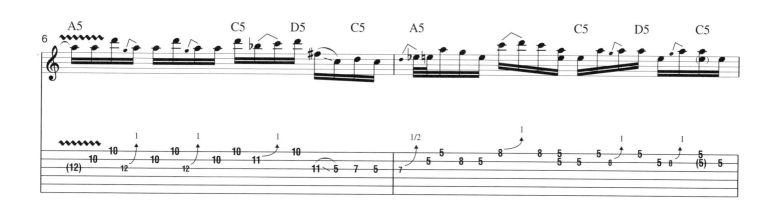

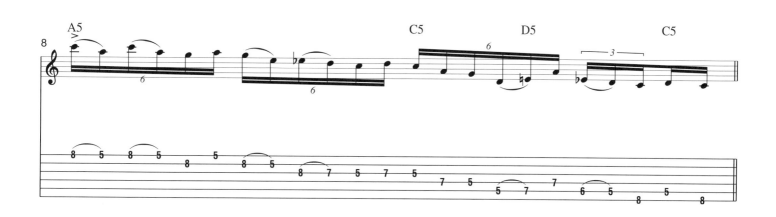

DUANE ALLMAN: with The Allman Brothers Band

STATESBORO BLUES
From *At Fillmore East* (Capricorn)
Words and Music by Willy McTell

Legendary blues/rock guitarist Duane Allman contributed greatly to the genre, his most formidable gift being his magnificent slide guitar playing. Technically, he was second to none; his use of right- and left-hand muting techniques lent his slide work a clarity and precision that had simply never before been approached. But in Duane's case, his brilliant technique functioned only as a vehicle for his soulful, expressive musical voice to be heard. Duane Allman set a standard on slide guitar that will continue to inspire for many years to come.

Duane's masterfully controlled phrasing and vibrato are exemplified by *Fillmore* tracks like "Statesboro Blues" and "Done Somebody Wrong." Stated Allman, "I heard Ry Cooder playing slide, and I said, 'Man, that's for me.'" Using primarily a two-pickup 1961 Gibson SG/Les Paul Standard—chosen for the double-cutaway design, which allows easy access to the upper regions of the fretboard—Duane wore a small glass Coricidin bottle (Coricidin is a cold medication) on his ring finger. He often played slide in open tunings, generally open E (low to high: E–B–E–G#–B–E) and open A (E–A–E–E–A–C#–E), and also played slide in standard tuning on songs such as "Dreams" and "Mountain Jam."

When playing slide, Duane fingerpicked exclusively, using his right thumb, index, and middle fingers to pluck the strings. A major element in the uniqueness of his sound was his right-hand muting techniques: while one finger picked a string, the other two were used for muting, resulting in a clear articulation.

Figure 17–Intro

On "Statesboro Blues," Duane's guitar is tuned to open E (low to high: E–B–E–G#–B–E). Customarily, slide guitarists will tune the guitar to the key of a given song, so that when the open strings are strummed—or the slide is placed across the twelfth fret—the *tonic* (the chord relative to the song's key) is heard.

In this case, Duane uses open E tuning for a song in D, so the majority of his licks are played at the tenth fret, one whole step below the twelfth. His licks are based on a scale that is a hybrid of D minor pentatonic (D–F–G–A–C) and D major pentatonic (D–E–F#–A–B) which is formed when playing all of the notes at the eighth and tenth fret of the A string through the high E string (he does not use the low E string). He will, of course, occasionally venture higher or lower on the fretboard, such as in measures 3, 5, 10, etc.

One of the trickiest things about playing slide is learning to execute vocal-like vibrato. Be sure to keep the slide parallel with the frets, and move back and forth (higher and lower) on the string in equal increments. Lightly rest the remaining fingers behind the slide across all of the strings. The thumb should rest on the back of the neck and be used as a fulcrum.

Dickey Betts's rhythm guitar part has been included here as well, and is very simple and straightforward. He begins with the repeated band figure based on D minor pentatonic and supplies the "Chuck Berry" root–5th–root–6th chords for the backing rhythm guitar figure through the verses and behind Duane's solo sections.

Fig. 17

Gtr. 1: Open E tuning:
(low to high) E–B–E–G♯–B–E

Intro 0:07-0:47

steady gliss.

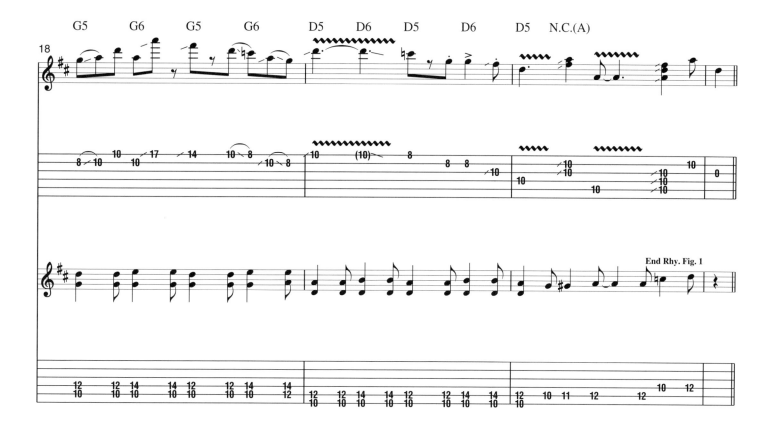

Figure 18–First Verse

During the verses, Duane adds little licks in the spaces left by brother Gregg's vocal. These licks are based on the same D minor/major pentatonic hybrid scale. Notice his subtle yet expressive use of grace notes throughout, such as those heard in measures 4 and 8. The lick across measures 11 and 12 begins with a typical Elmore James "Sweet Home Chicago" phrase, followed by an equally well-known Duane Allman twist of pulling the slide back a fret or two as the lick progresses from the higher to the lower strings.

Fig. 18

First Verse 0:47-1:09

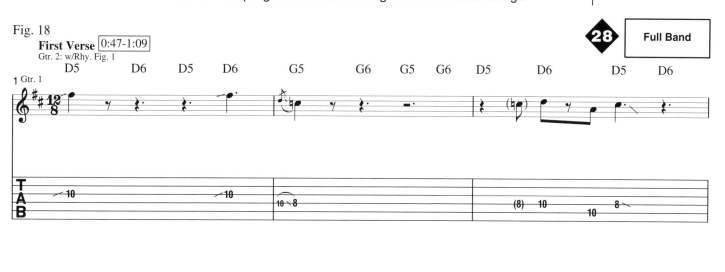

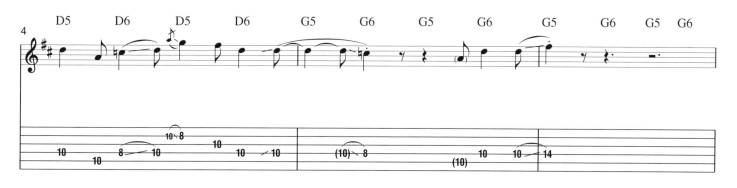

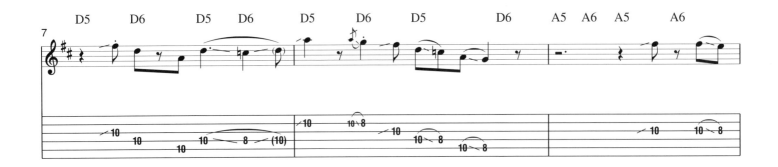

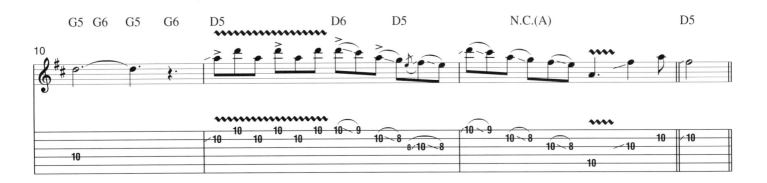

Figure 19–Duane's Solo, First Chorus

For his first twelve-measure chorus of soloing, Duane stays "parked" at the tenth fret for virtually the entire time; he only ventures higher—one octave higher, to the twenty-second fret—in the very last measure. Like all of the best blues guitarists, his improvised lines are very melodic and deceptively simple. Everything he plays seems so perfect, logical, and *easy*; it is only when one tries to replicate his playing that the realization is made that it only *sounds* easy.

29 Featured Guitar:
Gtr. 1   meas. 1-12

30 Slow Demo:
Gtr. 1   meas. 1-12

Fig. 19

Solo 1:32-1:55

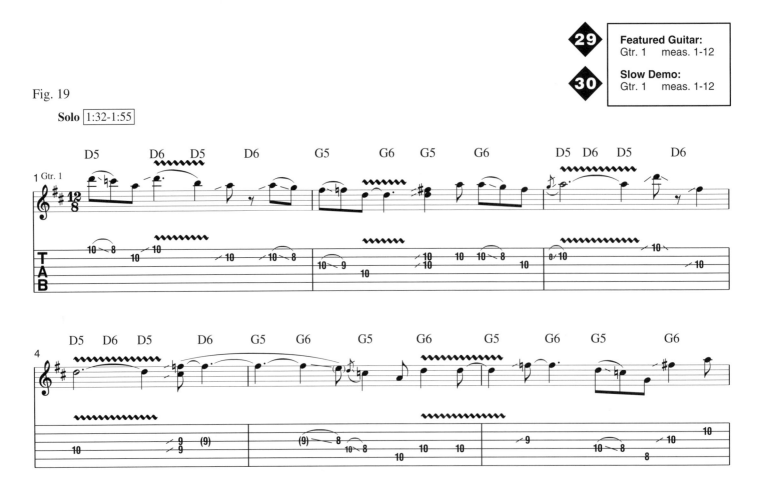

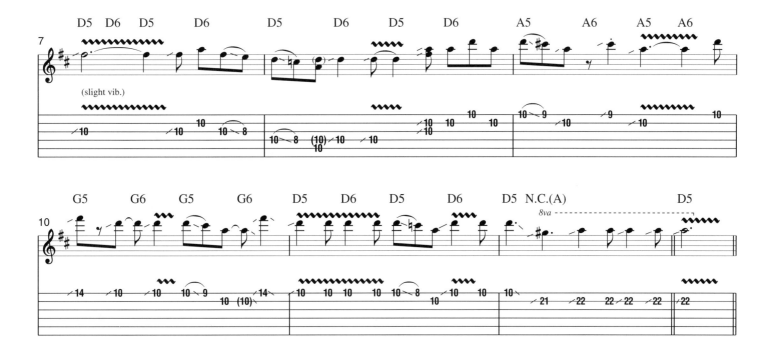

Figure 20–Duane's Solo, Second Chorus

The entire second chorus of Duane's solo is played one octave higher than the first, residing primarily between frets 20 and 22. When playing this high on the fretboard, it can be difficult to maintain the proper slide position of staying parallel with the frets; there is a tendency to bend the wrist slightly and find oneself in misalignment.

The most difficult lick in this chorus falls in measures 9 and 10: Duane moves very quickly, in even eighth notes, between the twentieth and twenty-second frets, fingerpicking all of the notes. Picking cleanly *and* keeping all of the notes in tune, while properly executing the occasional slides into the high A notes, is a task and will take diligent practice to master.

31 **Featured Guitar:**
Gtr. 1   meas. 1-12

32 **Slow Demos:**
Gtr. 1   meas. 1-12

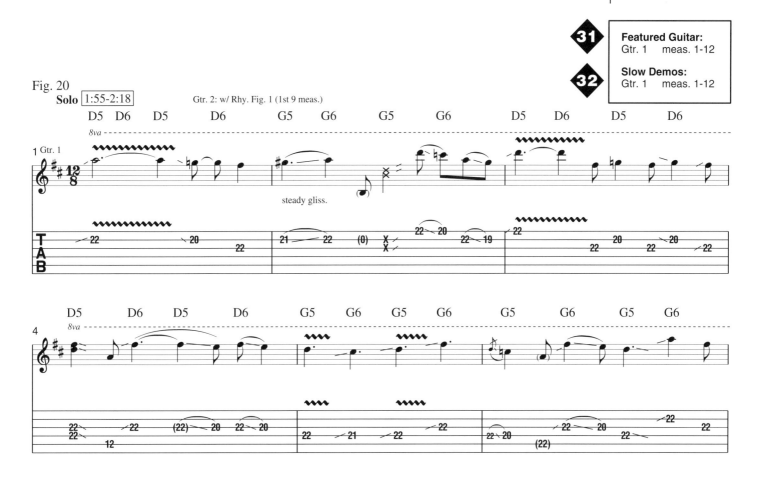

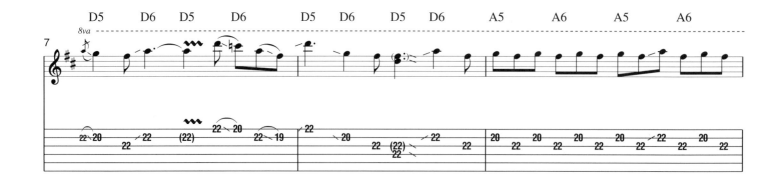

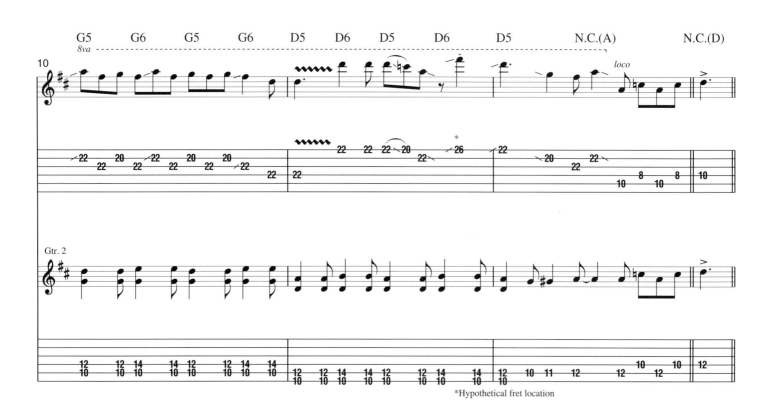

*Hypothetical fret location

WHIPPING POST
From *At Fillmore East* (Capricorn)
Words and Music by Gregg Allman

"Whipping Post" holds the unusual distinction as one of the most requested songs in rock; it has become a joke for people to yell out "Whipping Post!" at shows in which there is little or no chance of the artist playing the song. Perhaps this is because on the original recording, when Duane is introducing the song, someone yells out "Whipping Post!," and he says, "You guessed it!"

"Whipping Post" is a towering achievement in rock, as the Allmans used it as a vehicle to explore their unique and multi-faceted approach to band improvisation. On a nightly basis, the Allman Brothers would push the limits of rock music by bringing in elements of all of the styles that influenced them, including jazz, funk, R&B, blues, and bluegrass. It was through this musical cross-pollination that the Allmans created a "rock" sound that was totally new—one that still sounds fresh today.

Figure 21–Intro

"Whipping Post" begins with Berry Oakley's solo bass guitar figure, played over alternating measures of 6/8 and 5/8. Duane (Gtr. 1) enters in measure 5, playing a guitar figure that mimics Oakley's bass line. These licks are based on A minor pentatonic (A–C–D–E–G). Duane's lick is articulated with steady hammer-ons and pull-offs and is a bit tricky to execute smoothly. Duane repeats this figure through the entire intro.

Dickey Betts (Gtr. 2) enters at measure 7, playing a lick that is a take-off on Duane's lick. It is played one octave higher, utilizing the same basic melodic "shape," but is made up of fewer notes.

33 Full Band

Fig. 21

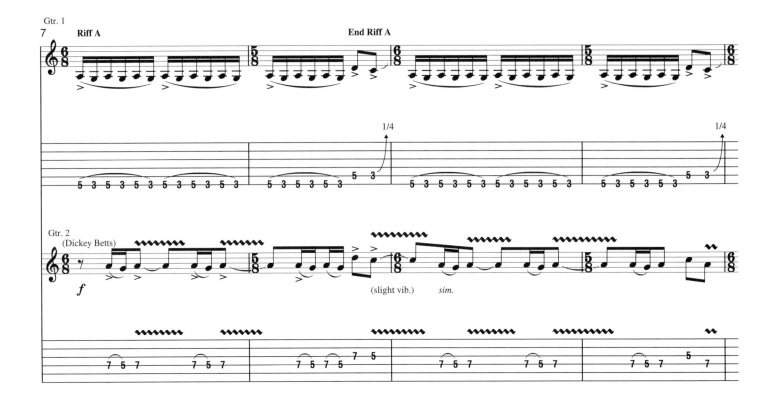

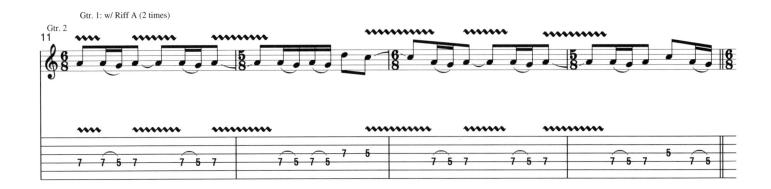

Figure 22–First Verse and Pre-Chorus

The verse section of "Whipping Post" is sixteen measures long and is played in straight 6/8 time. During this section, Dickey (Gtr. 2) supplies the chords, while Duane (Gtr. 1) plays in a less structured way, adding single-note licks and octaves in measures 7 and 8. Dickey's rhythm part is based on ascending and descending triadic chord forms played over an A pedal tone, supplied by Berry's bass line. The chords are Am, Bm/A, and C/A.

At the pre-chorus, Dickey hits sustained D7 and E7 chords, while Duane launches into solo bursts. In the first two measures of the pre-chorus (D7), his lines are based on D minor pentatonic (D–F–G–A–C); in the second two measures (E7), his lines are based on E minor pentatonic (E–G–A–B–D). In the first measure, Duane executes a *rake* as he slides up to F# (string 3/fret 11), sounded with a down-pick, followed by down-picks of A (string 2/fret 10) and D (string 1/fret 10). A rake is performed by dragging the pick across the strings in one motion; in this case, drag the pick from the G string, across the B string, and through the high E string.

Fig. 22

First Verse 0:14-1:14

*Am7

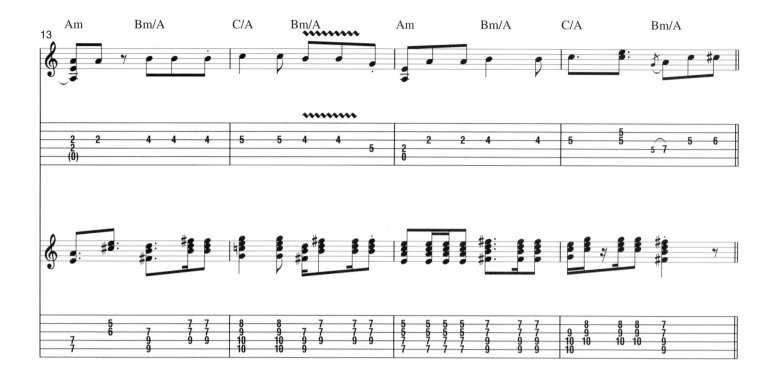

Pre-Chorus 1:07

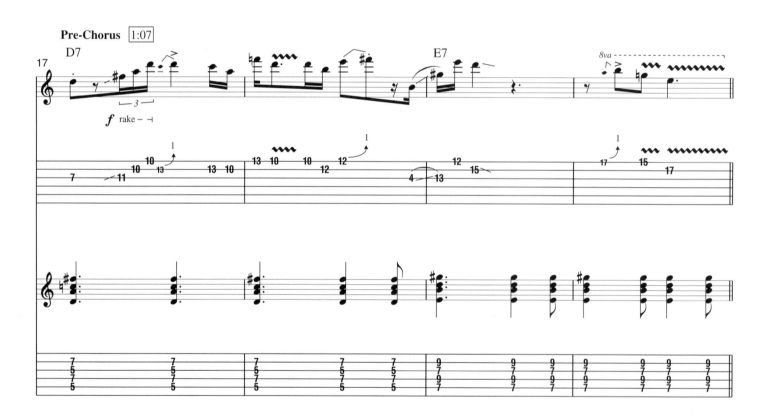

Figure 23–Chorus

The "Whipping Post" chorus features one of the many harmonized figures employed by Duane Allman and Dickey Betts. Dickey (Gtr. 2) plays the melody, based on A Mixolydian (A–B–C#–D–E–F#–G), while Duane (Gtr. 1) harmonizes Dickey's melody a 3rd higher, staying diatonic (within the key) to A Mixolydian. Notice that Duane articulates his lick slightly differently every time.

The section ends in the last two measures with a lick based on A minor pentatonic that is played in octaves: Duane plays the high lick in thirteenth position, while Dickey plays the lower lick in fifth position.

Fig. 23

Chorus 1:14-1:32

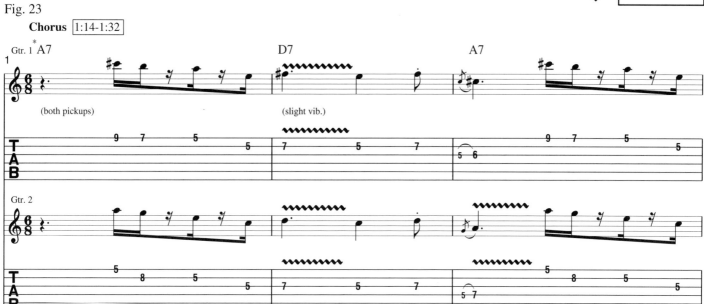

*Chords played by kybd.

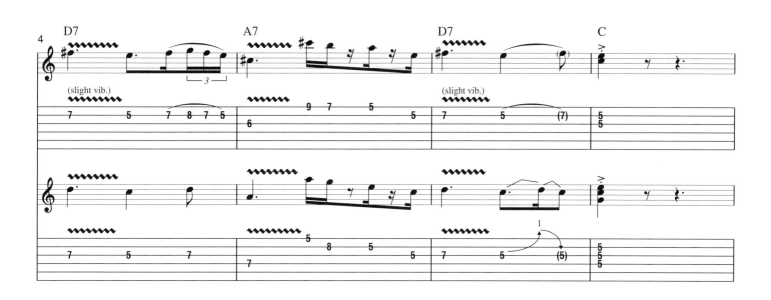

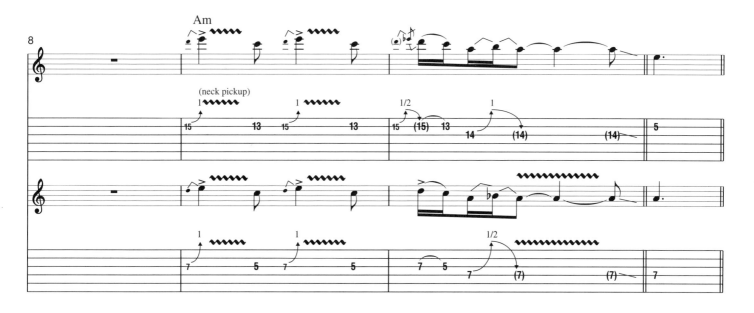

Figure 24–Duane's Solo, Pt. 1

As a means of instruction, Duane's lengthy solo has been segmented into two parts; the first segment represents measures 1–16 (illustrated below), and the second represents measures 17–36.

Duane's guitar solos are played over the verse chord progression of Am–Bm/A–C/A–Bm/A, performed by Dickey. Duane's lines are based on the A Dorian mode (A–B–C–D–E–F♯–G) in measures 1–6; his modal approach to soloing on this song was inspired by listening to jazz greats like trumpeter Miles Davis and saxophonist John Coltrane.

Duane's lines are very fluid, even when they are somewhat difficult to execute, as in measures 7–12, where he continually permutates one basic melodic shape based on A minor pentatonic. Duane sticks with A minor pentatonic through the rest of this excerpt. One of the most striking elements of this solo is how comfortable Duane sounds improvising in the 6/8 time signature.

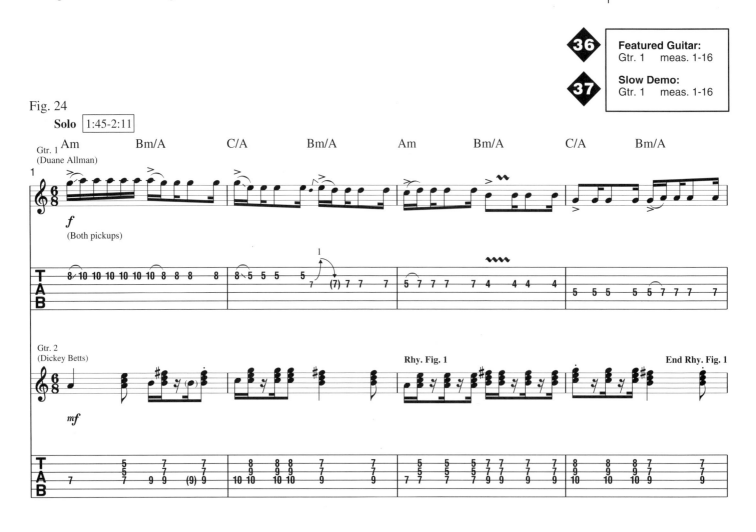

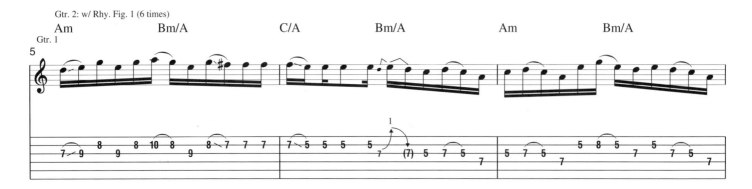

44

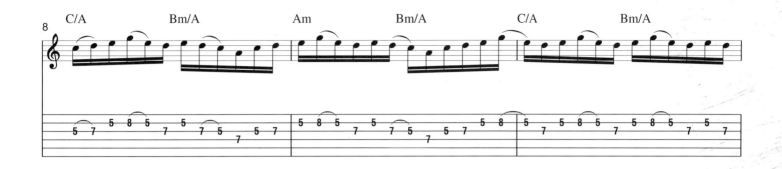

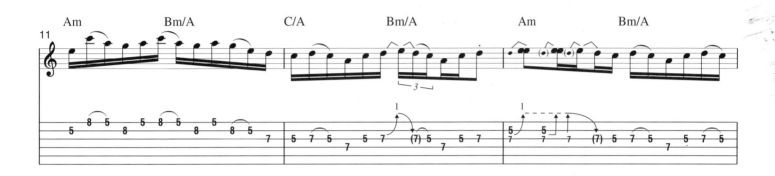

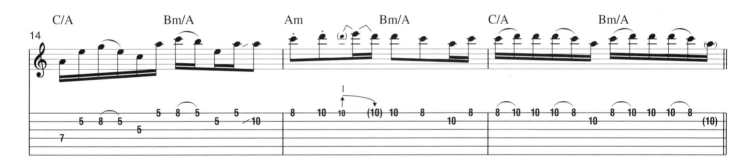

Figure 25–Duane's Solo, Pt. 2

In measures 1–9 of this example, Duane's improvised lines remain based on A minor pentatonic, and his phrases are very bluesy. In measure 10, he returns to the modal approach, again relying on A Dorian. In measures 17 and 18 of this example, Duane plays a fast pull-off riff on the G and D strings: fretting with the ring and index fingers, he rapidly pulls off from the fourth fret to the second fret to the open string, alternating between the G and D strings. In measures 19 and 20 of the example, he plays an ascending lick which is revisited, in a different rhythm, later in the song.

38 Featured Guitar:
Gtr. 1   meas. 1-21

39 Slow Demo:
Gtr. 1   meas. 1-21

Fig. 25

2:11-2:43

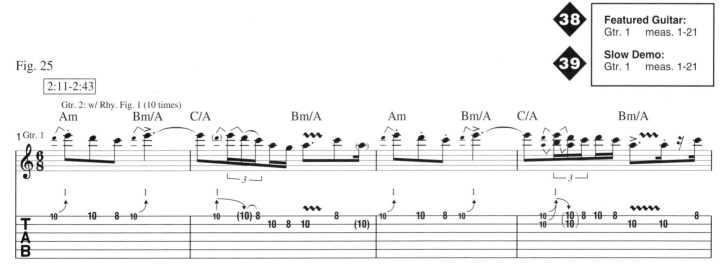

THE STUMBLE
From *A Hard Road* (London)
Words and Music by Freddie King and Sonny Thompson

In the spring of 1966, twenty-one-year-old guitar hero Eric Clapton left John Mayall's Bluesbreakers to start a little trio of his own, to be called Cream. Peter Green is the man then faced with the unenviable position of filling Clapton's rather large shoes.

As it turns out, no one better could have been chosen for the job. Green's playing on his Bluesbreakers debut, *A Hard Road*, is every bit as forceful and self-assured as his predecessor. He displays a complete understanding of the styles of Freddie and B.B. King while communicating a spirit of his own indicative of the spirited British blues of the era. *A Hard Road* even includes one of Green's better-known instrumentals—the beautifully haunting, "The Supernatural." By 1967, Green left Mayall to form what would become one of rock's biggest supergroups, Fleetwood Mac. Green is also the composer of "Black Magic Woman," made into a huge hit by Carlos Santana.

Figure 26–Theme (Head)

"The Stumble" is one of the most interesting of the many great instrumentals written by blues guitar legend Freddie King. It is a sixteen-measure form which begins on the IV chord (A) in the key of E and proceeds through this unusual, deceptively complex progression: IV–I–IV–V–I–IV–♭V°–I–VI–II–V–I–IV–I–V. In the key of E, that translates to: A–E–A–B–E–A–B♭°–E–C♯–F♯–B–E–A–E–B. Within the blues genre, that's a lot of chords.

Over this progression, Freddie wrote a melody that closely relates to the chord progression. The melody begins over the IV chord with a line based on E major pentatonic (E–F♯–G♯–B–C♯), and the notes he chooses (B, C♯, E, and F♯) are also common to A major pentatonic (A–B–C♯–E–F♯). In measure 2, the melody switches to E minor pentatonic (E–G–A–B–D), which sets up the chord change to E. The major 3rd of E (G♯) is included—as in measure 4—to strengthen the E dominant sound.

In measure 6, the melody switches to a line based on B minor pentatonic (B–D–E–F♯–A), which sets up the chord change to B. E minor pentatonic is returned to in measure 9, followed, in measures 10–12, with a shift to E major pentatonic. Measures 13 and 14 feature the signature "sliding 6ths" riff that is the song's trademark; Freddie used this same lick to great effect in his other classic instrumental, "Hideaway." The melody wraps up in the last two measures with a return to E minor pentatonic and a stock I–V "blues turnaround" lick.

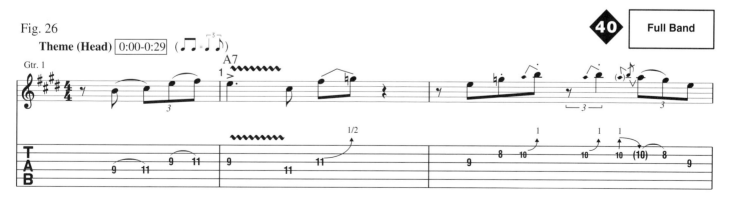

Fig. 26

Theme (Head) [0:00-0:29]

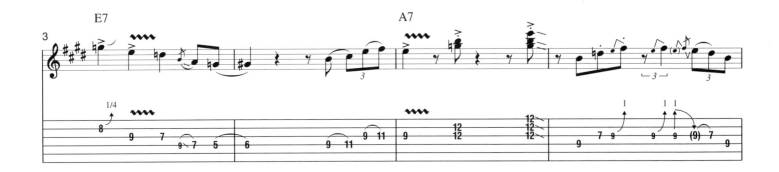

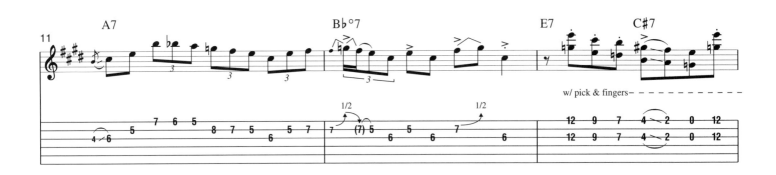

Figure 27–Solo, First Chorus

Peter Green begins his solo with crisp, concise phrases based on E minor pentatonic through the first five measures. Brief reference is made in measure 3 to the E blues scale (E–G–A–Bb–B–D) with the presence of Bb. In measures 6 and 7, he incorporates E major pentatonic, returning to E minor pentatonic is measures 9–12 for an absolutely blazing lick, delivered in steady eighth-note triplets and built from unusual but very effective phrasing. The entire four-measure lick is fretted with the ring and index fingers only and may require some work to sound as smooth as the way Peter performs it.

In measure 14, Green offers another standard "blues turnaround" type of lick, as pairs of notes descend chromatically on the A and D strings.

Figure 28–Solo, Second Chorus

On this second chorus of soloing, Green reveals his mastery of the Freddie King style, as his first eight measures replicate the phrasing, touch, and tone which earmark Freddie's sound. But this in no way diminishes the impact of Green's own musical personality; as reverent as this solo may be, his lines are saturated with his own distinct *attitude.*

For the first ten measures of this chorus, Green sticks with E minor pentatonic, incorporating many "ghost bends" within the phrases. (For a complete explanation of ghost bends, see the "Badge" solo section.) In measures 11 and 12, he shifts to E major pentatonic, which is well balanced against the surrounding E minor pentatonic licks. Measure 15 features the same descending turnaround lick played in measure 14 of his first chorus of the solo, starting this time on beat 2 instead of beat 1.

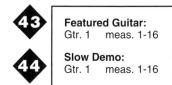

Featured Guitar:
Gtr. 1   meas. 1-16

Slow Demo:
Gtr. 1   meas. 1-16

Fig. 28

Solo, Second Chorus | 1:24-1:51 |

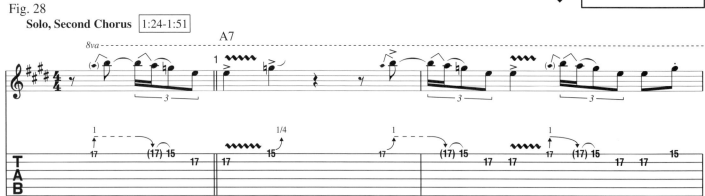

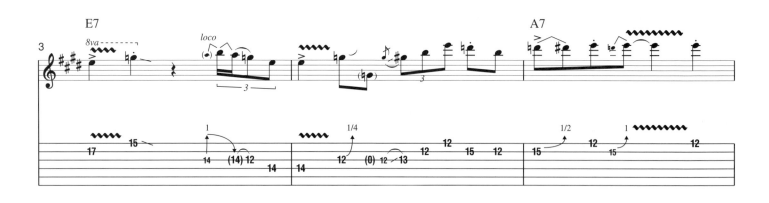

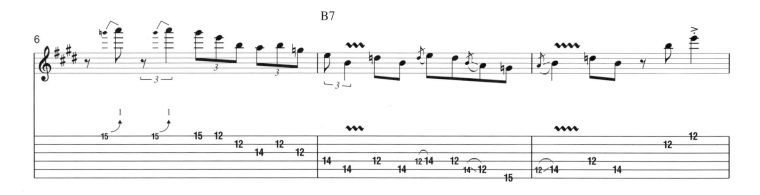

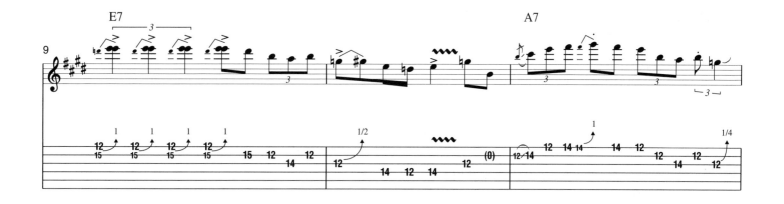

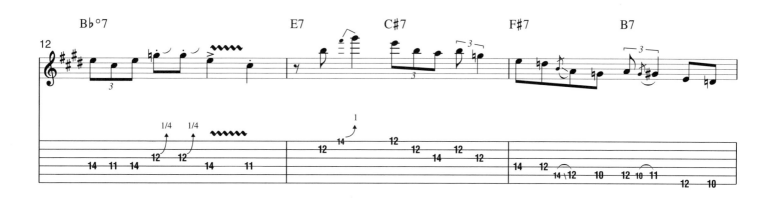

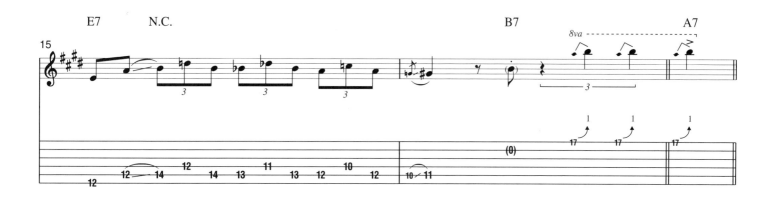

SOMEDAY, AFTER AWHILE
From *A Hard Road*

Words and Music by Freddie King and Sonny Thompson

This is truly one of Freddie King's greatest songs, and this Bluesbreakers recording rivals the original for power and pure blues feeling. Peter Green displays his ability to build intensity through succinct phrasing and masterful articulation; for fans of British blues, this is surely one of the genre's greatest performances.

Figure 29–Intro

Like the previous example, "The Stumble," this song is a 16-bar blues and utilizes a I–VI–II–V chord progression. In the key of F, that translates to: F–D–G–C, with all of the chords played as dominant sevenths. The intro is eight measures long and is identical to the second half (last eight measures) of the verse section.

Peter begins his intro solo with lines based on F major pentatonic (F–G–A–C–D), switching to F minor pentatonic (F–Ab–Bb–C–Eb) in measures 3–7. Notice, in measures 5 and 7, the inclusion of A natural (the major 3rd of F), which serves to strengthen the dominant seventh sound.

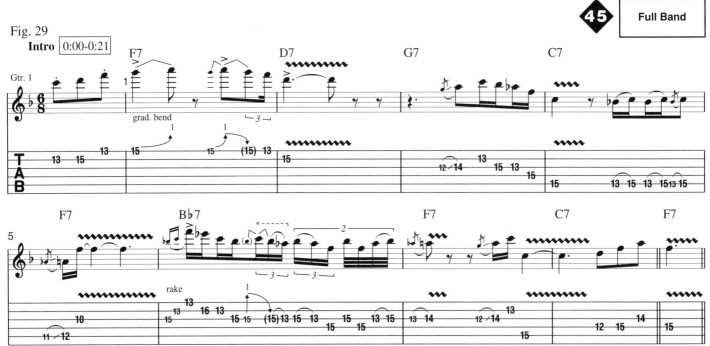

Fig. 29
Intro [0:00–0:21]

* Play slightly behind the beat

Figure 30–Verse

During the verse section, Green begins with sparse rhythm guitar and graduates to "answering" John Mayall's vocal phrases with improvised guitar licks. In measures 1–4, Peter plays sliding three-note chords. When voiced in twelfth position (the starting point), the implied harmony is F9; when slid up to fourteenth position, the implied harmony is F13. In measures 5–8, Green plays lines based on F minor pentatonic, switching to F major pentatonic in measures 9 and 10. Peter sticks with F minor pentatonic until the very last measure of the section, where he switches back to F major pentatonic and plays essentially the same riff with which he started the song. One of my favorite licks in this section is the one in measure 14, where Peter winds snaky F minor pentatonic lines down in first position.

Fig. 30

Verse 0:21-0:59

46 Full Band

Figure 31–Solo

Green takes a short solo on this song—it is only one chorus (sixteen measures) long—but it is packed with gem-like blues licks all the way through. He begins with F major pentatonic and in measure 2 uses "ghost bends" beautifully, moving between a high B♭ (the 4th) and A (the major 3rd). In measure 4, he shifts to F minor pentatonic with the inclusion of the major 3rd (A) and sticks with this scale for the remainder of the solo. For the most part, his phrasing is slow and deliberate, and he displays his expert vibrato liberally. Notice also his pointed staccato phrasing in measures 11 and 12. He wraps the solo up in measures 13 and 14 with a fast, idiosyncratic lick that is rhythmically complex; play through it slowly and scrutinize the slow version to get a clear grasp of it.

As usual, Green's tone, touch, phrasing, and articulation are right on the money—something to aspire to when learning to play this solo.

Figure 32–Bridge

During this section, Green adds forceful rhythm guitar based on major triads. In measures 1–4 of this section, he alternates Bb (Bb–D–F) and Eb (Bb–Eb–G) triads; in measures 5–7, he alternates F (F–A–C) and Bb (F–Bb–D) triads; in measures 9–12, he alternates G (G–B–D) and C (G–C–E) triads. Green ends the section in the last two measures with a C octave figure that ascends chromatically (one fret at a time) in the final measure.

Fig. 32

Bridge 1:37-2:15

HEY JOE
From *Are You Experienced?* (Reprise)
Words and Music by Billy Roberts

Following Eric Clapton's smashing impact on the world of guitar playing in 1966, Jimi Hendrix picked up the ball and *blasted* into an entirely different universe. Upon his arrival in England, Jimi wanted nothing more than to meet Eric; when Eric first heard Jimi play (at Polytechnic of Central London, sitting in with Cream), Eric is alleged to have said, hands shaking, "Is he really *that* good?" In just a matter of weeks, all of the UK was aware of a new guitar hero, and his name was Jimi Hendrix.

"Hey Joe" is a song Jimi had been playing in the clubs of New York while still a scuffling musician. Curiously, it was the song Animals bassist Chas Chandler had wanted to record as a producer; all he needed was the right artist. When Chas happened upon Hendrix performing in an East Village club, Jimi had already worked up his own stunning arrangement of the song. In December of '66, "Hey Joe" was released as the Jimi Hendrix Experience's first single, backed with Jimi's first original composition, "Stone Free."

Figure 33–Intro and First Verse

Hendrix begins this song with an unaccompanied three-measure figure. A blues lick based on E minor pentatonic in measure 1 is followed in measure 2 by an E major chord and sliding two-note figures. On beats 3 and 4 of measure 3, Jimi plays another lick based on E minor pentatonic, setting up the verse chord progression of C–G–D–A–E. This "cycle of 5ths" progression continues through the remainder of the tune. Jimi's complete mastery of R&B/soul rhythm guitar is revealed in this verse section, as he seamlessly combines two- and three-note chord voicings, voice leading, and single-note figures. This primary rhythm guitar part—as well as the secondary, accompanying rhythm part—are performed with a crystal-clear tone.

Of note are the chord voicings Jimi uses for the G and A chords, in which sixth-string root notes are fretted with the thumb. Using his thumb to fret these low root notes allowed Jimi the opportunity to use his other fingers to embellish the chords with bits of improvisation. The aforementioned secondary rhythm guitar supplies dead-string accents on beats 2 and 4, which serve to support the backbeat snare drum accents. This guitar also adds fills based on E minor pentatonic and is played with an "out-of-phase" pickup selection: the guitar's toggle switch is set between the middle and bridge pickups, yielding a thin, bright tone.

Fig. 33

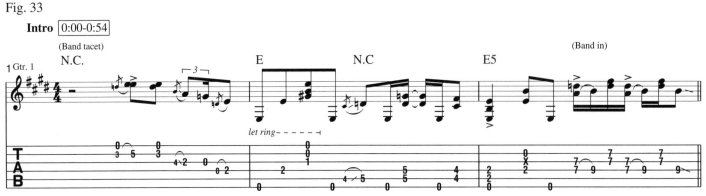

Figure 34–Solo

The "Hey Joe" solo is regarded as one of Jimi's best; he would quote this solo nearly verbatim whenever playing the song live. This solo is based on E minor pentatonic (E–G–A–B–D), with the exception of the brief F♯ notes that appear in measure 7. A very cool moment in the solo is when Jimi (inadvertently?) plays an open D string in measure 5, beat 3, on the second sixteenth note. The solo ends in measures 9 and 10 with the time-honored chromatically ascending lick that serves to link all of the chords in the progression together.

After careful study of the solo, thoroughly investigate the rhythm guitar part, too. Like everything Jimi played, this part is full of invention and spirited creativity.

51 **Featured Guitar:**
Gtr. 2   meas. 1-12

52 **Slow Demo:**
Gtr. 2   meas. 1-12

KILLING FLOOR
From *BBC Sessions* (Experience Hendrix/MCA)
Words and Music by Chester Burnett (Howlin' Wolf)

From the very inception of his life as a guitarist, Jimi Hendrix was a blues fanatic. Records by B.B. King, Albert King, Elmore James, John Lee Hooker, and Muddy Waters were listened to over and over again, supplying Jimi with a priceless education in the work of the masters. Right at the top of the heap was Chester Burnett, a.k.a. Howlin' Wolf, who, along with Muddy Waters, set the template for modern blues—and, in the process, all rock music of the future—with his classic fifties and sixties Chess recordings.

Wolf's original version of "Killing Floor" was released in 1964 (included on *The Real Folk Blues*), and Jimi welcomed the song into his own repertoire immediately. At his landmark American debut at the 1967 Monterey Pop Festival, Hendrix opened with his white-hot rendition of "Killing Floor." Prior to that performance, The Jimi Hendrix Experience recorded the song for the BBC on March 28, 1967, to be aired April 1, 1967. None of Hendrix's BBC recordings were officially released until 1998's *BBC Sessions*, which includes the version represented here.

Figure 35–Intro

First and foremost, remember to tune the guitar down one half step (low to high: Eb–Ab–Db–Gb–Bb–Eb) when playing this song along with the recording. Jimi kicks off this wild rendition with six measures of unaccompanied guitar, performing a dense and complex rhythm part that revolves around A root notes sounded either as single notes (on the fourth string/seventh fret or sixth string/fifth fret), or in pairs as an A octave. The A notes on the fourth string are usually fretted with the ring finger, and the A notes on the sixth string are fretted with the thumb. The C note on the sixth string is fretted with the pinky. This is an intricate and tricky rhythm part to recreate; start slowly and strive to have all of the elements clearly in your mind before working it up to tempo.

Measure 7 of this example functions as the beginning of the twelve-measure form of the song, at which point Jimi doubles the bass guitar figure. In measures 1–4, 7–8, and 11, all of Jimi's parts are based on A minor pentatonic (A–C–D–E–G). In measures 11–12 (over D), the figure is based on D minor pentatonic (D–F–G–A–C), and in measure 15 he plays a "Chuck Berry" root-5th/root-6th rock 'n' roll rhythm part over E.

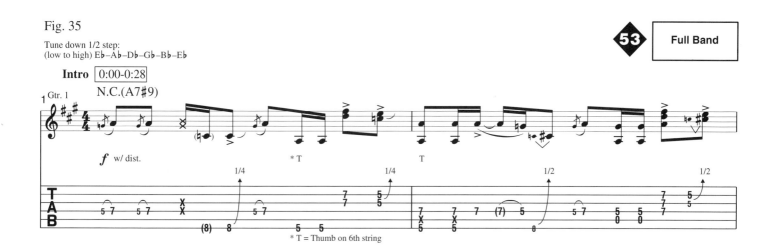

Fig. 35

Tune down 1/2 step:
(low to high) Eb–Ab–Db–Gb–Bb–Eb

Intro 0:00-0:28

* T = Thumb on 6th string

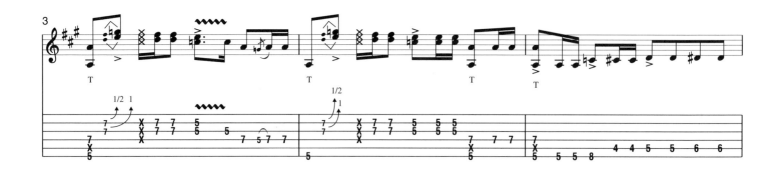

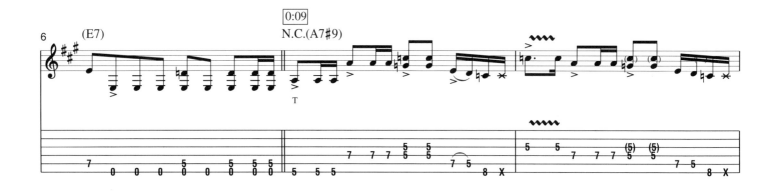

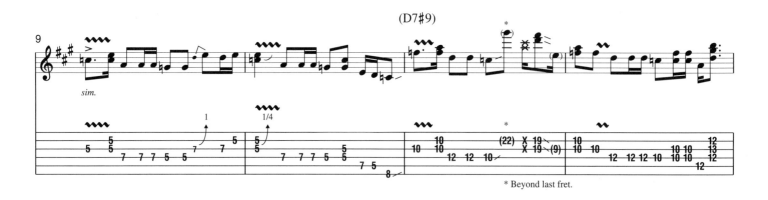

* Beyond last fret.

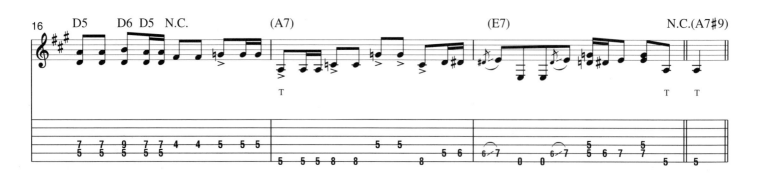

Figure 36–First Verse

Jimi's rhythm guitar part during this section is very similar to that played during the twelve-measure section of the intro; study and compare both to see how Jimi improvised with the basic form. He ends this section with an E7#9 chord, a chord which he'd used to great effect in his song "Purple Haze" from *Are You Experienced?*.

54 Full Band

Fig. 36

First Verse 0:28–0:47

Figure 37–Solo, First Chorus

Jimi begins the solo section with the "Killing Floor" signature lick: on the G and high E strings, double-stop (two-note) figures a 6th apart are played over each chord in the progression. Over A in measures 1–4 and 7 these double stops are based on A Mixolydian (A–B–C#–D–E–F#–G); over D in measures 5, 6, and 10 the double stops are based on D Mixolydian (D–E–F#–G–A–B–C); over E in measure 9 the double stops are based on E Mixolydian (E–F#–G#–A–B–C#–D). These double-stop licks are staples of blues guitar and can be heard on countless other classic blues recordings.

In the last two measures, Jimi plays a blazing, intricately-phrased A minor pentatonic lick, quickly shifting up to A minor pentatonic in fifteenth position in the next measure, which sets up his second solo chorus.

Fig. 37

Solo, First Chorus 1:05-1:23

64

Figure 38–Solo, Second Chorus

Jimi begins his second solo chorus with four measures of double-stop figures that allude primarily to A minor pentatonic, with a brief reference to A Mixolydian. These phrases accentuate a "quarter-note triplet" feel, wherein three quarter notes are evenly spaced across two beats. Measure 5 begins with big, Albert King-style one-and-a-half- and two-step bends, followed with a B-to-C♯ bend, fretted with the middle finger, at the end of measure 6. Using the middle finger for this bend allows use of the pinky to fret the high F♯ notes (first string/fourteenth fret) in measure 7. By measure 9, Jimi has worked his way back down to A minor pentatonic in fifth position; his ability to seamlessly shift positions is a clear indication of Jimi's true mastery of blues guitar.

57 Featured Guitar:
Gtr. 1   meas. 1-12

58 Slow Demo:
Gtr. 1   meas. 1-12

Fig. 38

* Played slightly behind the beat.

RICHIE BLACKMORE: with Deep Purple

LAZY
From *Machine Head* (Warner Brothers)
Words and Music by Ritchie Blackmore, Ian Gillan, Roger Glover, Jon Lord and Ian Paice

With the release of 1972's *Machine Head*, which included the smash hit "Smoke on the Water," Deep Purple staked their claim as rulers of the kingdom of heavy metal. The album went on to achieve multi-platinum status, and today *Machine Head* is rightfully revered as one of the greatest rock albums of all time. The fact that the album was recorded with mobile gear in the rooms and hallways of a hotel only enhances its infamous reputation.

Virtuoso guitarist Richie Blackmore delivers some of the most incendiary playing of his career on *Machine Head*; an excellent example of his unique, mind-boggling style is the twisted blues shuffle, "Lazy."

Figure 39–Theme (w/opening solo)

"Lazy" is essentially a 12-bar blues shuffle, but Deep Purple experiments with the form here and there. Following Jon Lord's extended keyboard solo, the initial presentation of the song's theme enters at the 1:43 mark and is presented as an eight-measure figure within a sixteen-measure form. Richie Blackmore introduces this theme, based on the F Blues scale (F–A♭–B♭–B–C–E♭), in measures 1–8.

In the following eight measures of this section, Richie plays delicate solo lines, again based on the F blues scale, reflective of the influence of B.B. King. A true Blackmore trademark is the use of *staccato* phrasing as in measures 9–10 and 13–14.

Fig. 39

* Chords played by organ.

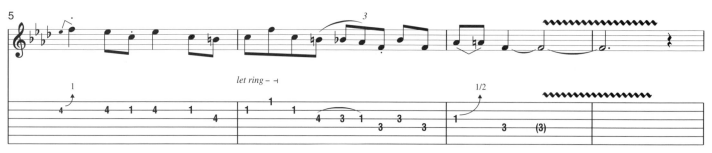

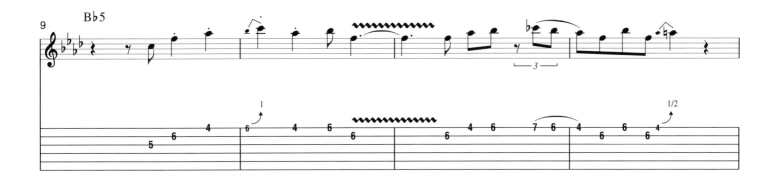

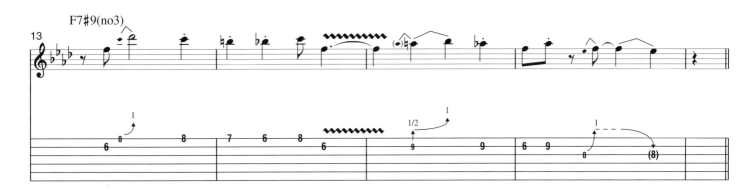

Figure 40–Main Theme

Immediately following the above intro, the "Lazy" main theme is played as a band figure and is lengthened to a twelve-measure form. Points of interest are the single measure of 2/4 (measure 4) and the simplification of the theme in measure 6. In measures 9–12, the primary riff has been transposed to the V chord (C), based here on the C blues scale (C–E♭–F–G♭–G–B♭).

Full Band

Fig. 40

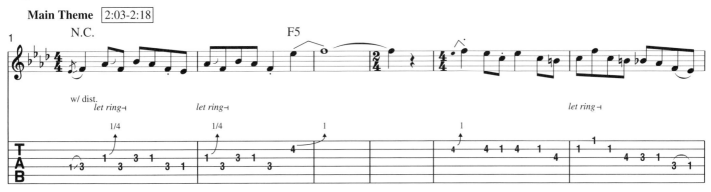

Figure 41–First Solo, First Chorus

The many facets of Richie Blackmore's genius as a guitarist can be found within the first three choruses of his soloing on this song. His articulation is *stunning*: absolute precision is combined with authority, drive, attitude, soul, and, above all, impeccable musicality.

Blackmore begins with phrases based on the F blues scale and, in measure 5, expands the harmonic environment with the inclusion of D, which alludes to both F Dorian (F–G–Ab–Bb–C–D–Eb) and F Mixolydian (F–G–A–Bb–C–D–Eb). Measure 6 features a brief visit to F major pentatonic (F–G–A–C–D), followed by a return to F minor pentatonic (F–Ab–Bb–C–Eb) in measure 7 (notice the trill on the upbeat of beat 3). Across measures 9 and 10, Richie plays a slick hammer-on/pull-off lick based on the C blues scale over the Ab–Eb chord progression. The solo wraps up with a return to F minor pentatonic.

Richie supports the solo with a simple, bass-like overdubbed rhythm guitar figure for the I chord (F) and the IV chord (Bb). Over the Ab and Eb chords (played by the keyboards), he adds single notes. This rhythm part appears, with slight variations, behind the next two choruses of soloing as well.

61 Featured Guitar:
Gtr. 1   meas. 1-12

62 Slow Demo:
Gtr. 1   meas. 1-12

Fig. 41

First Solo, First Chorus [2:18–2:33]

68

Figure 42–First Solo, Second Chorus

This entire chorus is based on the F blues scale and again features some very slick and flashy articulation from Richie. There is an abundance of *legato* (smooth and connected) phrasing, via the deft use of hammer-ons, pull-offs, and slides. Try your best to make these lines sound the way he does; his control is consistently brilliant.

63 Featured Guitar:
Gtr. 1   meas. 1-12

64 Slow Demo:
Gtr. 1   meas. 1-12

Fig. 42

First Solo, Second Chorus   2:33-2:49

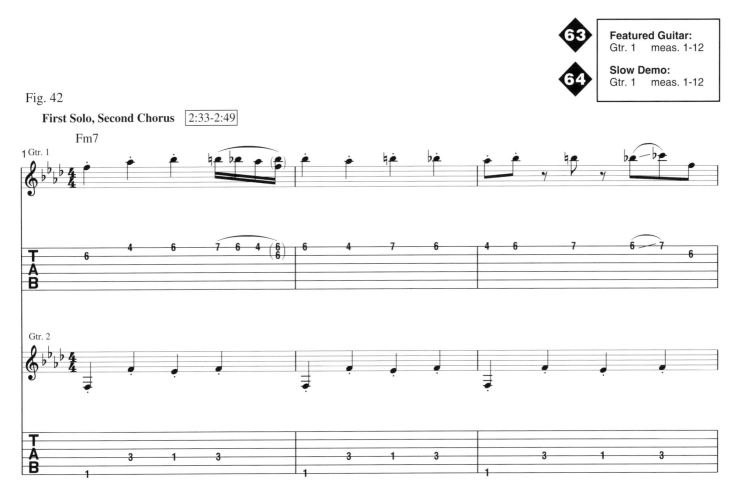

Figure 43–First Solo, Third Chorus

This chorus is by far the hardest of the three to perform. Blackmore's first phrase is played in an unorthodox way. He begins by sliding chromatically from C♭ to C on the G string, followed immediately by a B♭-to-A♭ pull-off on the D string, which can force a positional shift. Following the initial index-finger slide from C♭ to C, there are a variety of ways to finger this lick: 1) fret B♭ with the ring finger and pull-off to A♭ fretted with the index finger; 2) fret B♭ with the pinky and pull-off to A♭ fretted with the index finger; 3) fret B♭ with the pinky and pull-off to A♭ fretted with the middle finger.

Measures 3–9 may drive you crazy: using the index, middle finger, and pinky, Blackmore weaves a snaky, intricate line based on F Aeolian (F–G–A♭–B♭–C–D♭–E♭), with the inclusion of C♭ (B), the ♭5. Throughout these measures he repeatedly alternates between slides and pull-offs and brings hammer-ons into the mix in measure 3. The physical difficulty in recreating these lines stems from the fourth-to-fifth-fret slide on the G string—causing a positional shift—which anchors the majority of the licks. All of the licks in this section are phrased with an eighth-note triplet feel, except the last beat of measure 9, which brings a nice twist via the use of straight sixteenths.

65 Featured Guitar:
Gtr. 1   meas. 1-12

66 Slow Demo:
Gtr. 1   meas. 1-12

Fig. 43

First Solo, Third Chorus [2:49-3:04]

71

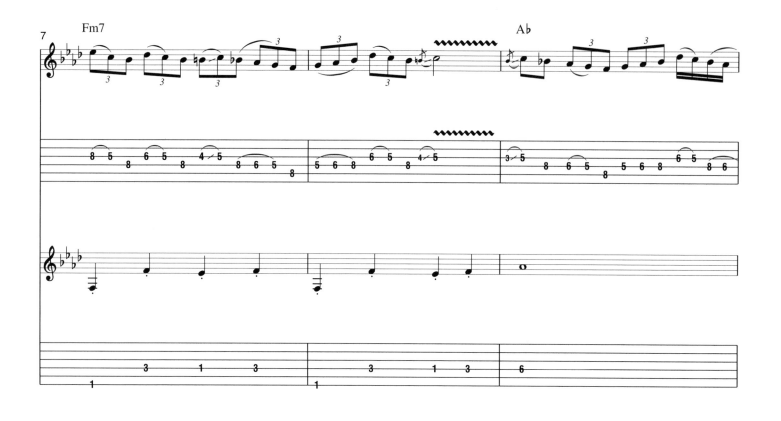

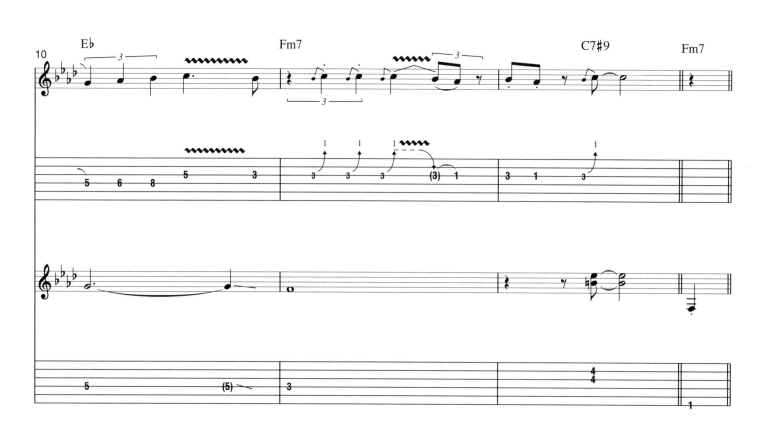

SMOKE ON THE WATER
From *Machine Head* (Warner Brothers)
Words and Music by Ritchie Blackmore, Ian Gillan, Roger Glover, Jon Lord and Ian Paice

There may have been a "No 'Stairway'" sign in the movie *Wayne's World*, but this Deep Purple classic may deserve the real top honors as "the lick most played by someone trying out a guitar in a music store." The song also deserves honors as one of the most heavily rotated songs in classic rock radio history, all for good reason: it's a great song, it features inspired performances from each band member, and, of course, it contains a perfectly conceived and executed guitar solo.

Figure 44–Intro

The song's main lick is first introduced here, unaccompanied. The lick is made up of pairs of notes a 4th apart; these notes represent the root and the 5th of a series of power chords: G5–B♭5–C5–G5–B♭5–D♭5–C5. The 5th is placed on the bottom ("in the bass") for these chords. The riff is based on the G blues scale (G–B♭–C–D♭–D–F). In the first and second endings, a full three-note G5 power chord is sounded.

Fig. 44

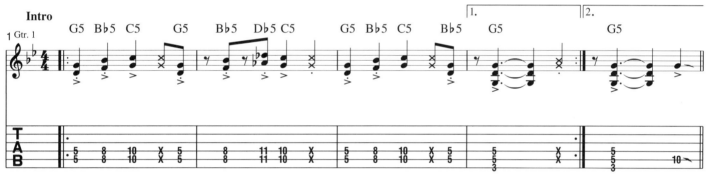

Figure 45–First Verse

The verse section is sixteen measures long and is comprised of a four-measure figure played four times. In the first, second, and fourth measures of most of these four-measure groups, a G5 chord is arpeggiated (played as single notes); in the third measure of each group, G5 is played for beats 1 and 2, and F5 is played for beats 3 and 4. The lone exceptions are when two-note pairs are played instead of single notes (measure 10, for example).

Fig. 45

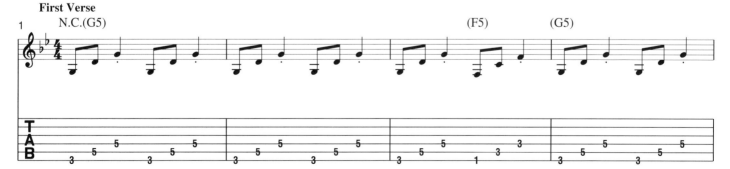

Figure 46–Chorus

The first six measures of this section introduce a new chord progression: C5–A♭5–G5. As in the verse section, Richie arpeggiates these power chords. The song's primary lick is then restated for measures 7–14.

69 **Full Band**

Fig. 46

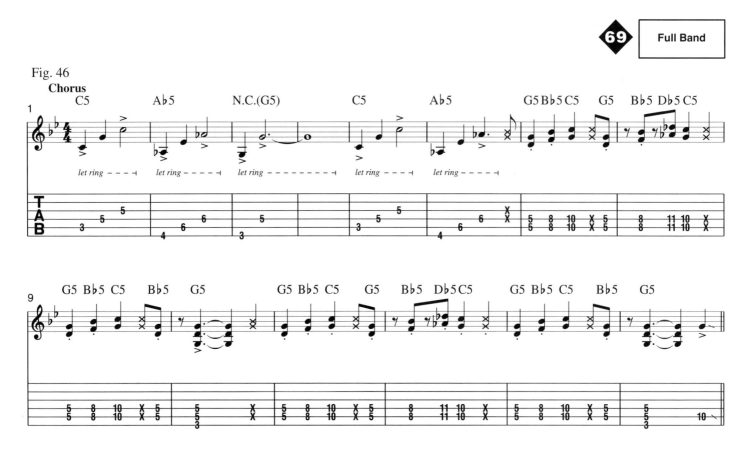

Figure 47—Solo

The solo section introduces an entirely different chord progression. The chords are based on the verse progression, but the section has been stretched out to twenty-four measures. A four-measure phrase—two measures of G5, followed by a measure of C5 and a measure of G5—is played four times, covering the first sixteen measures of this section. Measures 17 and 18 feature C5, followed by two measures over F (F5 and Fsus2, respectively). The last four measures of the section restate the song's main lick.

Blackmore begins the solo with lines based on G minor pentatonic (G–B♭–C–D–F), but quickly shifts to G Aeolian (G–A–B♭–C–D–E♭–F) by measure 3. His trademark staccato phrasing is in evidence once again, as well as his beautifully precise articulation. The hardest lick falls in measure 7, wherein fast, sixteenth-note-driven lines based on a combination of C Dorian (C–D–E♭–F–G–A–B♭) and the C blues scale (C–E♭–F–G♭–G–B♭) spill into G Aeolian. Similarly phrased licks are found in measure 11, based on a combination of G Dorian (G–A–B♭–C–D–E–F) and the G blues scale; and in measure 15, based on C minor pentatonic (C–E♭–F–G–B♭). Of note also is the subtle tremolo bar dip in measure 10.

One of the coolest moments, however, is the simplest to recreate. In measure 21, Richie flips the toggle switch to the bridge position, attaining a razor-sharp tone for the high C-to-D bent notes that cap off the solo.

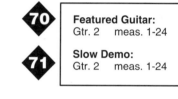

70 Featured Guitar:
Gtr. 2   meas. 1-24

71 Slow Demo:
Gtr. 2   meas. 1-24

Fig. 47

Solo

JEFF BECK

ROCK MY PLIMSOUL
From *Truth* (Epic)
Words and Music by Jeffrey Rod

Another guitarist faced with the unenviable position of replacing Eric Clapton during the mid-sixties "Clapton Is God" phase in England was the inimitable Jeff Beck, who took Eric's place in the neo-blues outfit the Yardbirds. Jeff wasted no time marking his territory; instead of following Clapton's "lead," Beck invented a whole new approach to rock guitar, immediately earning respect as a completely new, viscerally aggressive voice on the instrument.

By 1968, Jeff had formed his first group as a leader, featuring two of rock's future superstars—Rod Stewart on vocals and Ronnie Wood (Rolling Stones/Faces) on bass. The debut release of this band, *Truth*, is a crushing collection of irreverent hard blues/rock and is considered by some to be the strongest album of Jeff Beck's career.

Figure 48–Intro

"Rock My Plimsoul" is Jeff's twisted take on B.B. King's blues classic, "Rock Me Baby," which is a standard I–IV–V 12-bar blues. Beck plays two different guitar parts throughout this recording—one lead and one rhythm—and both parts display a swaggering self-confidence that is Beck's signature. Gtr. 2 represents the rhythm guitar part, which lays down a simple, bass-like figure made up of root notes and dominant 7ths for each chord in the progression.

On top of this rhythm part is a lead guitar part that essentially doubles the rhythm guitar for the first four measures and then launches into improvised lines based on B minor pentatonic (B–D–E–F♯–A). Notice the rich quality of Beck's vibrato: a good example is the E-to-F♯ bend at the end of measure 4, wherein the G string is fretted with the ring finger and bent up (towards the wound strings) and then vibratoed, followed by a gradual release and pull-off to D♯, the major 3rd. The section ends with an angry pick slide, as Jeff scrapes the pick slowly down the strings, pushing hard so that one can hear the pick passing each fret.

If you play along with the original recording of this song, you will notice that it has been sped up and sounds one quarter-tone sharp.

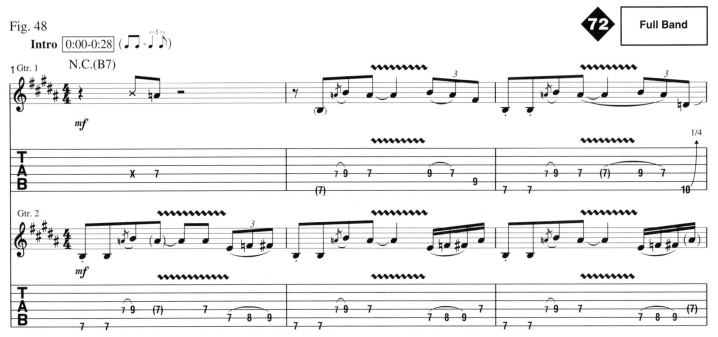

Fig. 48

Intro 0:00-0:28

Figure 49–First Verse

During this verse, both Gtrs. 1 and 2 play the basic rhythm part. Though there are very slight discrepancies between the two guitars, these parts have been arranged here for one guitar. Notice the slight variations in the basic lick as the section progresses.

73 Full Band

Fig. 49

First Verse 0:28-0:54

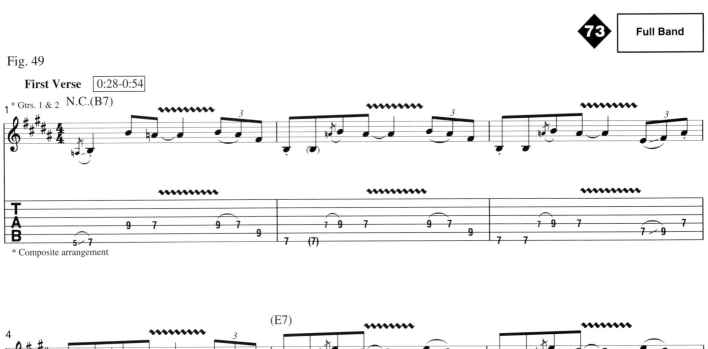

* Composite arrangement

Figure 50–Solo, First Chorus

The solo Beck devised for this song is nothing short of brilliant. It is powerful, irreverent, and bursting with soul. Measures 1–8 are primarily based on B minor pentatonic. Jeff begins the solo boldly with unison bends fretted on the G and B strings. Notes on the B string are fretted with the index finger, and notes on the G string are fretted with the ring finger and are bent up and vibratoed akin to the intro solo.

The bend and release in measure 4, which spills into measure 5, is fretted with the index finger, followed in measures 5–7 with fast, idiosyncratic phrasing. Study the slow recording of this solo for a clearer understanding of these complex phrases. At the end of measure 8, Jeff switches to a lick based on B major pentatonic (B–C♯–D♯–F♯–G♯) that culminates in measures 11–12 with *oblique* bends (while one note is bent, another is held stationary) phrased as quarter-note triplets.

The rhythm guitar part begins with an entirely different figure, but settles back into the basic rhythm figure by measure 3.

74 Featured Guitar:
Gtr. 1   meas. 1-12

75 Slow Demo:
Gtr. 1   meas. 1-12

Fig. 50

Solo, First Chorus [1:20-1:46]

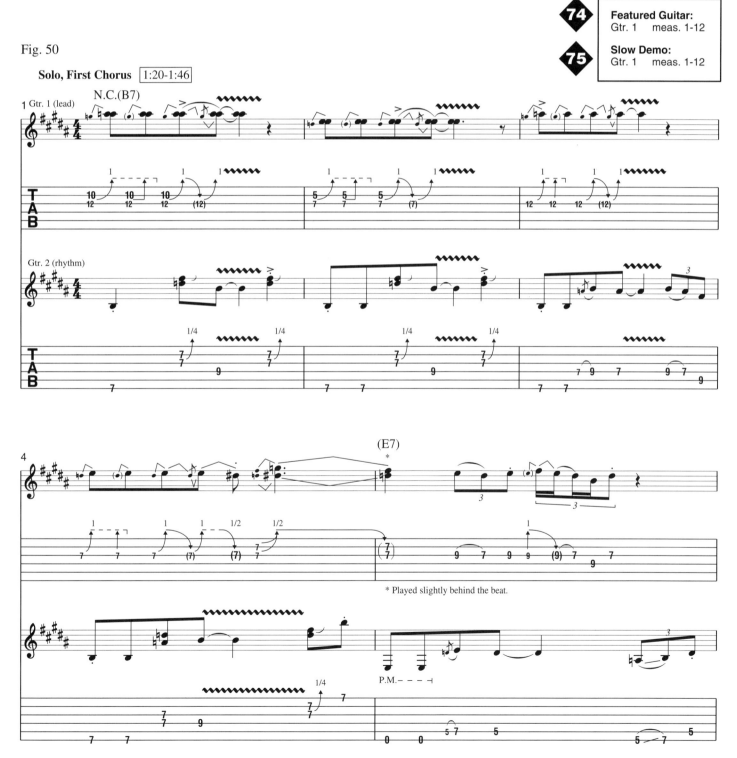

* Played slightly behind the beat.

81

* Played slightly ahead of the beat.

Figure 51–Solo, Second Chorus

This chorus of improvisation begins with the end of the phrase started in the last two measures of the previous chorus, based on B major pentatonic. Beck sticks with this scale through the first four measures; by the end of measure 4 and into measure 5, he performs a series of two-steps bends—A to a high C♯—on the B string at the twenty-second fret. The blazing lick that falls across the last two beats of measure 6 is essentially based on B minor pentatonic, with the brief inclusion of C♯; this is actually a permutation on a lick used often by B.B. King.

In measure 9, Jeff plays an expressive trill between high E and F♯ notes, slowing the trill down into steady sixteenths in measure 10. The solo ends with whole-step bends at the twenty-second fret of the high E string, followed by another aggressive pick slide.

Take notice of the rhythm guitar part during this second solo chorus, as Beck creates heightened tension by switching to a "harder-driving" rhythm figure.

76

Featured Guitar:
Gtr. 1   meas. 1-12

77

Slow Demo:
Gtr. 1   meas. 1-12

Fig. 51

Solo, Second Chorus   1:47-2:12

* Played slightly ahead of the beat.

* Played slightly ahead of the beat.

LET ME LOVE YOU
From *Truth* (Epic)

Words and Music by Jeffrey Rod

"Let Me Love You," another blues/rock masterpiece from *Truth*, clearly helped to define this style of music back in the nascent days of the genre. Though its structure is that of a standard 12-bar blues, it is performed with so much vibrant originality that it succeeds in transcending the form. Like "Rock my Plimsoul," if you play along with the original recording of this song, you will notice that it has been sped up and sounds one quarter-tone sharp.

Figure 52–Intro

This song kicks off with an evil-sounding low lick, played by the rhythm guitar (Gtr. 2), that is based on F♯ minor pentatonic (F♯–A–B–C♯–E). The majority of the improvisation in this song is based on this scale, along with the F♯ blues scale (F♯–A–B–C–C♯–E). Jeff's highly active rhythm guitar part does not establish any specific riff; instead, it is a completely improvised part that dynamically drives the rhythmic nature of the song. This part will require close scrutiny to recreate accurately.

Over this thick rhythm part, Beck plays relatively simple solo figures based primarily on F♯ minor pentatonic. In measure 7, he brings D♯ into the mix, and, in measures 8 and 9, accentuates the major 3rd (A♯). In measure 11, Jeff performs a high two-step bend (similar to those heard in "Rock My Plimsoul"), as he incorporates the F♯ blues scale. And like "Plimsoul," this intro solo ends with a similarly violent pick slide.

Fig. 52

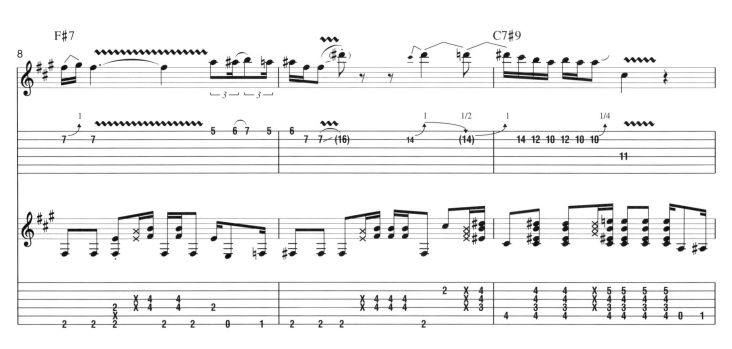

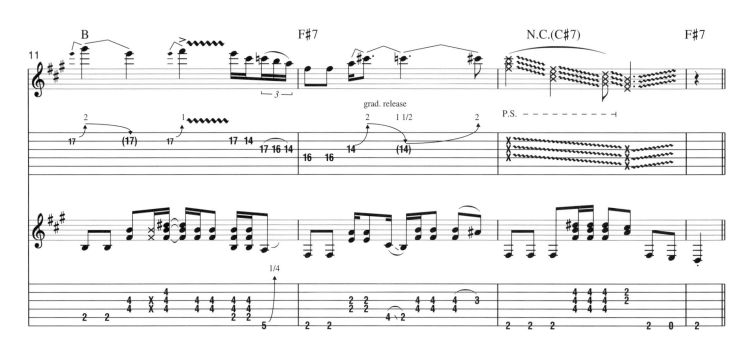

Figure 53–First Verse

The first verse also features two distinct guitar parts: Gtr. 2 supplies the basic rhythm figure, which revolves around dominant seventh voicings played for each chord in the progression. The only repeated "riff" played by this guitar is found in measures 3–4, 7–8, and 11–12 and supports the bona-fide "Let Me Love You" primary lick, played by Gtr. 1, which falls in those same measures and is based on the F♯ Mixolydian mode (F♯–G♯–A♯–B–C♯–D♯–E).

79 | **Full Band**

Fig. 53

First Verse | 0:33-1:02

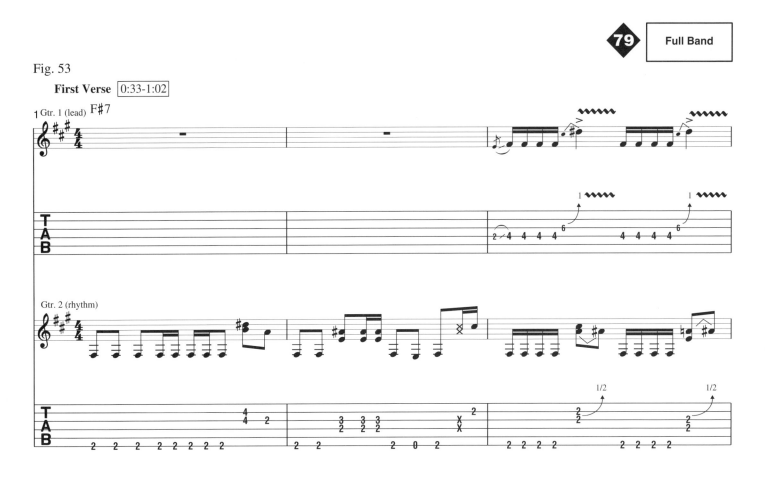

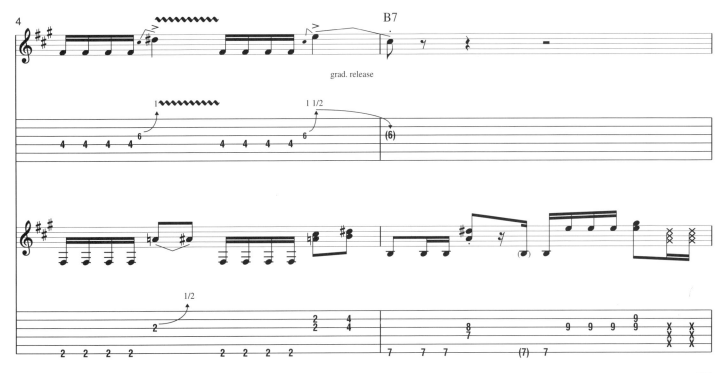

Figure 54–Solo, First Chorus

As a whole, Jeff Beck's solo in this song is truly one of the great moments in all of rock's recorded history. His two choruses of soloing overflow with a high-intensity musical spirit and irreverent nature—in other words, *flash*. The majority of his improvisations are based on the F♯ blues scale, and he gets things off to a rollicking start in measure 1 with a bizarre two-step bend from B to D♯. Playing two-step bends on the G string in fourth position will require some real hand strength and may take getting used to.

On the last beat of measure 2, Jeff begins the second phrase of his solo with a highly unusual phrase, making use of the open D string, followed by a melodic figure that "answers" the first phrase of the solo. In measures 5 and 6, he accentuates the use of "ghost bends" (notes which are bent before they are picked) and follows this in measures 7 and 8 with a brilliantly conceived and executed two-measure phrase based on sixteenth-note triplets.

Measures 9 and 10 feature "chordal" riffs, as the lines played here are built from standard fifth-string-root C♯ and B major chords. In measure 11, Jeff begins by pivoting off a low F♯, fretted with the thumb, and finishes the chorus with more aggressive licks based on F♯ minor pentatonic.

Give additional attention to the Gtr. 2 rhythm part, which is nearly as inventive and unpredictable as the solo.

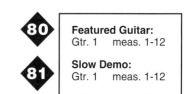

Featured Guitar:
Gtr. 1   meas. 1-12

Slow Demo:
Gtr. 1   meas. 1-12

Fig. 54

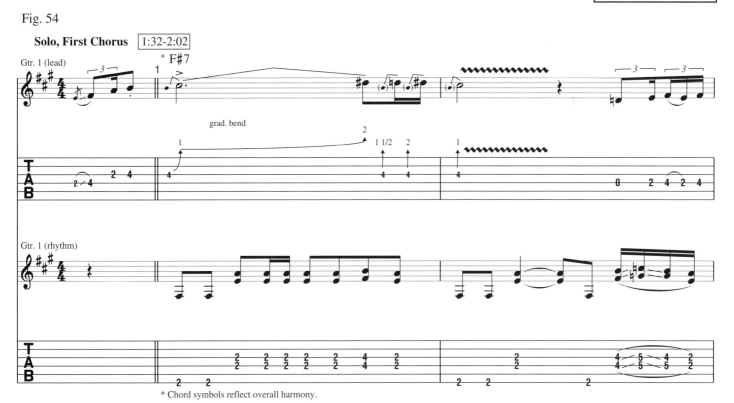

* Chord symbols reflect overall harmony.

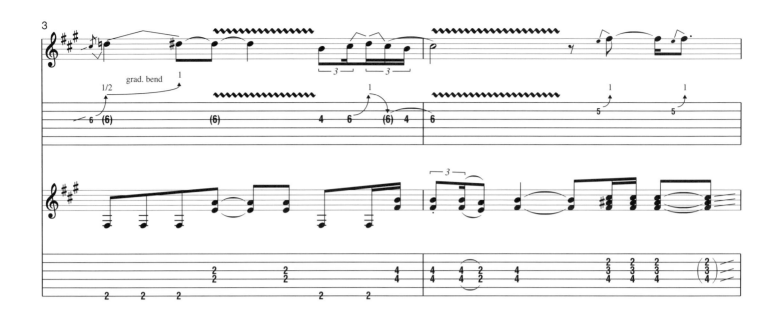

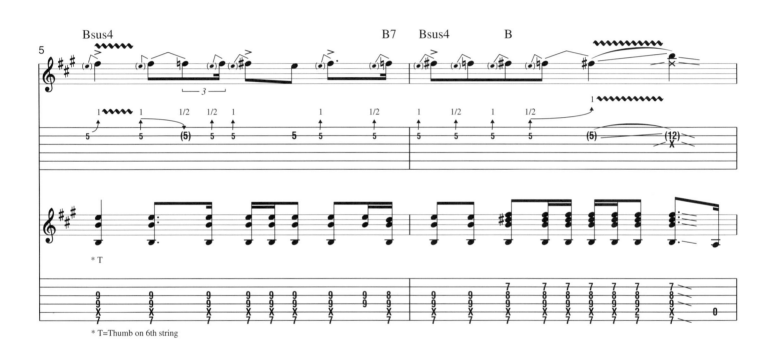

* T=Thumb on 6th string

Figure 55–Solo, Second Chorus

In this second solo chorus, Jeff spends the first nine measures "parked" in fourteenth position and plays lines based primarily on F♯ Mixolydian. He begins with "ghost bends" that are played staccato and delivers a clearly conceived melody across the first two measures. In measure 3, he plays a triplet lick on the top two strings, executing the pull-offs on the high E string with the pinky, middle, and index fingers. In measures 5 and 6, Jeff plays similar pull-off riffs, articulated the same way, on the B string.

In measure 9, Jeff briefly alludes to C♯ major pentatonic (C♯–D♯–E♯–G♯–A♯) over the C♯9 chord, followed by a shift up to sixteenth position to execute the high D♯/B voicing in measure 10. Beck rounds off the solo with a restatement (of sorts) of the song's primary lick.

As in the first solo chorus, Jeff's rhythm guitar part is hard-driving but very free. Compare the two choruses to get an idea of the scope of his imaginative powers.

Fig. 55

Solo, Second Chorus 2:03-2:33

LESLIE WEST: with Mountain and solo

MISSISSIPPI QUEEN
From *Mountain Climbing!* (Windfall)
Words and Music by Leslie West, Felix Pappalardi, Corky Laing and David Rea

In 1967, while still a teenager, New York native Leslie West was recording singles for Atlantic Records with his first band, The Vagrants; they actually released the soul classic "Respect" prior to the hit version by Aretha Franklin. Dismal sales forced the dissolution of the group, but not before Cream producer Felix Pappalardi got an earful of Leslie and decided to leave the producer ranks and join Leslie as a full-time performer. Together they formed Mountain, and on the strength of such songs as "Mississippi Queen," "Nantucket Sleighride," "Theme From an Imaginary Western," "Dreams of Milk and Honey," and "Never in My Life," are regarded as one of the heaviest rock bands ever.

Leslie West's signature tone came from Les Paul Juniors played through a Sunn PA head used as a power amp into Marshalls. This combination produced one of the fattest and heaviest rock tones ever heard. His slow, wide vibrato and succinct, melodic phrasing hugely influenced such guitar heroes as Eddie Van Halen and Randy Rhoads, among many others. Combined with his incredibly powerful singing voice, Leslie West has earned his place in rock history as one of its greatest legends. Mountain's biggest hit is the classic rock radio staple, "Mississippi Queen."

Figure 56–Intro

Following drummer Corky Laing's insistent opening cowbell figure, the "Mississippi Queen" primary riff is introduced at the end of measure 1 and into measure 2. This riff is based on E minor pentatonic.

"Mississippi Queen" is basically a 12-bar blues in the key of E, and measures 4 and 5 of the intro make reference to the V and IV chords of a 12-bar blues—B5 and A5, respectively—within a I–IV–V blues progression. The rhythm guitar part is played by two guitars in unison.

Over these chords, Leslie plays an intro solo based on E major pentatonic which is indicative of his style. The rock-solid melody is perfectly phrased and articulated, adorned with Leslie's immediately recognizable vibrato. These phrases stem from the blues, but are delivered with the venom of pure rock.

84 Full Band

Fig. 56

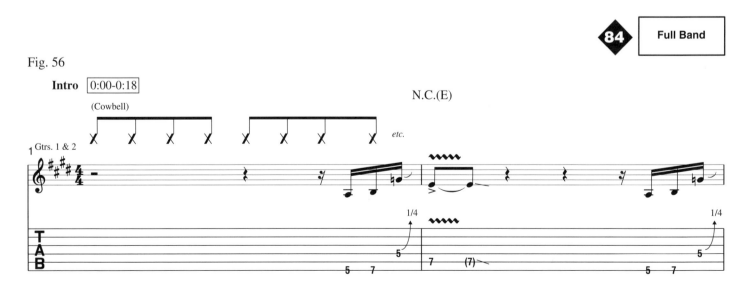

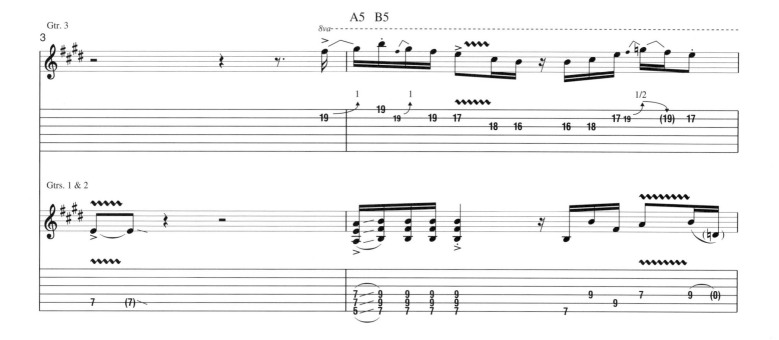

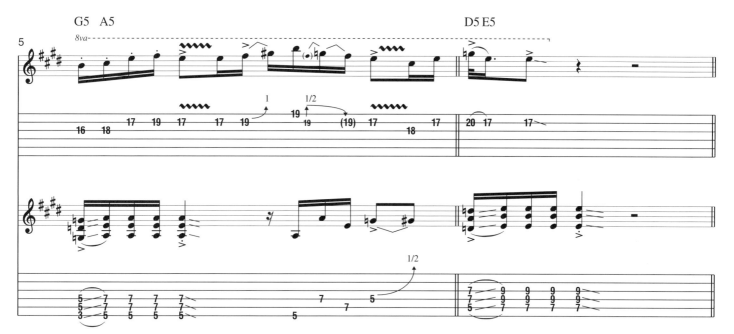

Figure 57–First Verse

The verse section breaks down to two rhythm guitars that play power chords in conjunction with single-note figures. The single-note figures relate directly to each chord in the progression: over E, they are based on E minor pentatonic; over A, they are based on A minor pentatonic; over B, they are based on B minor pentatonic.

Fig. 57

First Verse 0:18-0:58

85 Full Band

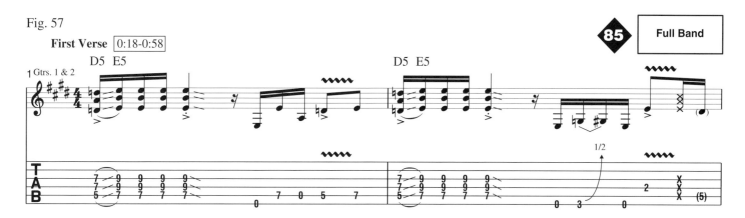

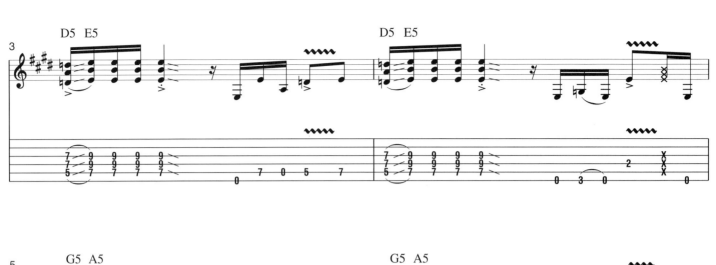

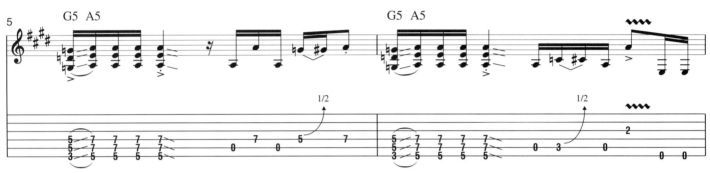

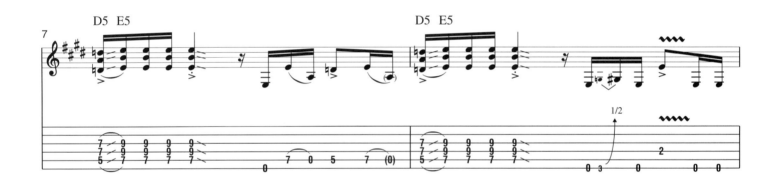

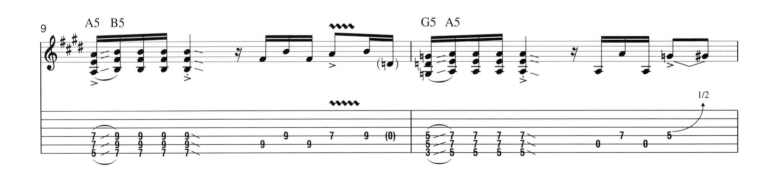

Figure 58–Solo

The guitar solo is played over the verse's chord progression and rhythm guitar part. In measures 1, 2, and 4, Leslie's lines are based on E major pentatonic, with a brief visit to E minor pentatonic in measure 3. Over A5 in measures 5 and 6, he returns to E minor pentatonic (with the inclusion of G♮) and then effectively switches back to E major pentatonic in measure 7 with the return to the root chord (E5). He then sticks with this scale through the rest of his solo. Alternating between minor and major pentatonic is a technique employed by all of the "kings" of blues guitar, emulated to great effect by Leslie West and Eric Clapton.

Of special note in this solo are: 1) the quick pull-off lick, from high G to E, on beat 4 of measure 7—Leslie had used this same lick at the end of his intro solo, fretting the G with the ring finger and pulling off to the index finger; 2) the series of high "ghost bends" in measure 8—other than the very first note, each of these pitches is attained by precisely pre-bending the string. Study the slow version of this solo for a clearer picture on how to execute this figure.

86 Featured Guitar:
Gtr. 3   meas. 1-11

87 Slow Demo:
Gtr. 3   meas. 1-11

Fig. 58

Solo 1:40-2:14

DREAMS OF MILK AND HONEY

From *Mountain* (Windfall)

Words and Music by Felix Pappalardi, John Ventura, Leslie West and Norman Landsberg

Prior to the release of Mountain's proper debut, *Climbing!*, which featured the well-known line-up of West, Pappalardi, Corky Laing, and keyboardist Steve Knight, Leslie and Felix had hooked up with drummer N. D. Smart and keyboardist Norman Landsberg for Leslie's solo debut, called *Mountain*. This classic blues/rock album contains many formidable tunes and performances; one of the stellar highlights is the massive "Dreams of Milk and Honey," which contains one of the greatest guitar solos of Leslie West's career.

Figure 59–Intro and First Verse

The "Dreams of Milk and Honey" intro sets up the song's basic five-measure progression, which is subsequently repeated through the verse section. During the verse, this five-measure pattern is played four times. This pattern is slightly unusual in that it incorporates a measure of 2/4 (measure 2) to accommodate the song's primary lick; this lick is based on E minor pentatonic (E–G–A–B–D).

During the intro, Gtr. 2 supplies the backing rhythm part, while Gtr. 1, in measures 1 and 2, doubles the rhythm guitar one octave higher. In measures 3–4, Gtr. 1 plays solo lines based on E minor pentatonic. Once again, notice Leslie's smooth articulation and succinct melodic phrasing. Throughout this tune, Leslie utilizes what Clapton refers to as the "woman tone": with the guitar set on the bridge pickup (or when using a single-bridge-pickup guitar like a Les Paul Junior), the tone control is turned either all the way off or is barely on (set at 1 or 2). This yields a thick, "creamy" tone that became a trademark for both Eric and Leslie.

The first two times the primary rhythm figure is played during the verse, Gtr. 1 drops out (measures 6–15). Gtr. 1 re-enters in measure 16 and supplies solo lines that "answer" the vocal; these lines are based on E minor pentatonic until measures 21–23. Across the last two measures of the section in measures 24–25, Leslie switches to E minor pentatonic and then back to E major pentatonic.

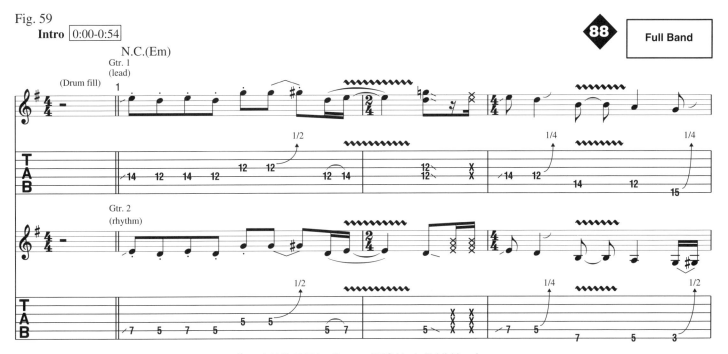

Fig. 59
Intro 0:00-0:54

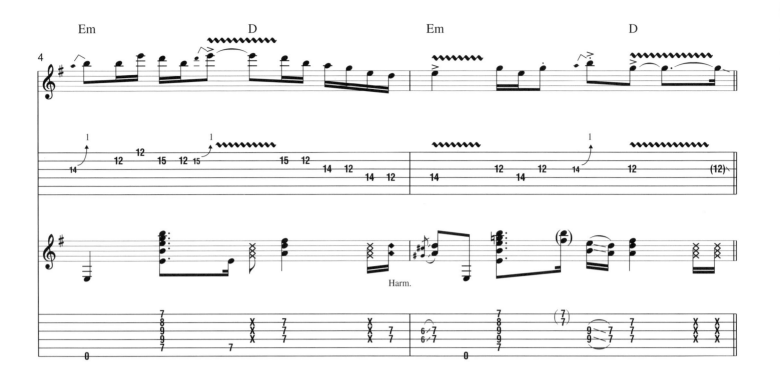

First Verse

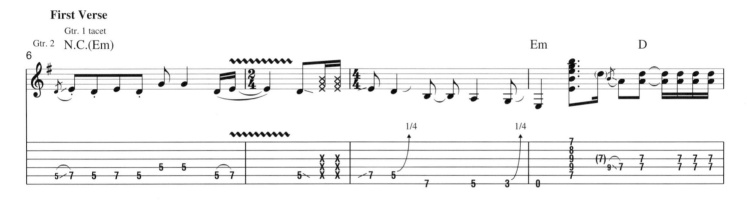

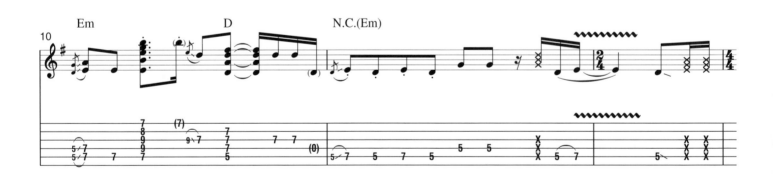

Figure 60–Chorus

Like the verse, the chorus section utilizes changes in time signature: the section alternates measures of 3/4 and 4/4 three times, which covers the first six measures of the section, and then ends with another measure of 4/4. Though this is certainly unusual, it sounds perfectly natural within the context of this progression. Gtr. 2 plays the rhythm part, while Gtr. 1 tacets (does not play) until the final two measures, wherein Gtr. 1 adds solo figures based on G minor pentatonic (G–B♭–C–D–F) over the C chord. The song then launches straight into the solo section.

Fig. 60

Chorus 0:55–1:09

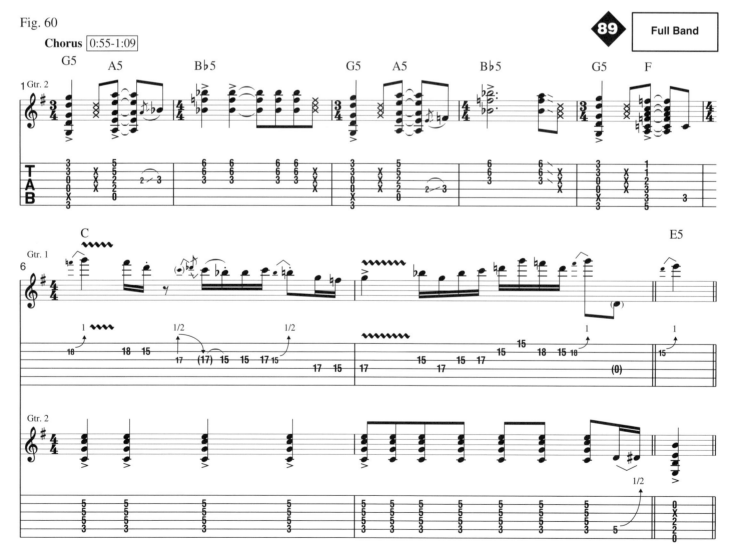

Figure 61–Solo

The solo section introduces a new chord progression, E5–G5–E5–A5–G5–E5, which is two measures in length and is played three times. This is followed by a riff that alludes to two measures of A5. Taken together, this creates an eight-measure form that is then played twice, creating a solo section sixteen measures in length. In the initial two-measure rhythm figure, power chords voiced within the first three frets are used; the two-measure lick in measures 7–8, which alludes to A5, consists of the open A string combined with A and G notes played on the D string.

West uses minor pentatonic scales exclusively for this solo. Over the E5 tonality in measures 1–6, he uses E minor pentatonic; over the A5 tonality in measures 7–8 and 15–16, he uses blues. As stated previously, this is a true gem of a solo; the melodic content, phrasing, touch, and tone are magnificent, and the performance is equally inspired. None of the lines are *technically* difficult, but, akin to recreating the playing of the blues masters, delivering these lines with the forceful assuredness and intense vibe of Leslie West is no easy task.

90 Featured Guitar:
Gtr. 1   meas. 1-16

91 Slow Demo:
Gtr. 1   meas. 1-16

Fig. 61
Solo 1:09-1:47

STEVIE RAY VAUGHAN: with Double Trouble

PRIDE AND JOY
From *Texas Flood* (Epic)
Written by Stevie Ray Vaughan

Of all the legendary blues/rock guitarists covered in this book, Stevie Ray Vaughan is the only one to have emerged during a time other than the sixties or seventies. Stevie Ray released his landmark debut, *Texas Flood*, in 1983, and with its release a new guitar hero had arrived. Thoroughly versed in the playing styles of everything from the classic blues of the fifties and early sixties to the adventurous rocked-up blues of the late sixties and early seventies, SRV burst onto the scene as a fully-formed *guitar monster*. Stevie deserves credit for single-handedly turning the world at large back on to a style of music and approach to guitar playing that, at the time, was considered out of vogue.

Texas Flood was recorded in just three days, and that sense of immediacy is captured within the album's ten tracks. *Texas Flood's* centerpiece is Stevie's hard-drivin' shuffle, "Pride and Joy."

Figure 62–Intro

"Pride and Joy" is a standard 12-bar blues shuffle based on a I–IV–V chord progression in the key of E: E7–A7–B7. Remember that Stevie tunes his guitar down one half step (low to high: Eb–Ab–Db–Gb–Bb–Eb). For the intro, Stevie kicks things off with a four-measure unaccompanied figure that recalls blues guitar legend Lightnin' Hopkins. Stevie begins by sliding into an E note on the second string which is played in unison with the open high E string. Measure 2 presents a classic "country blues" lick based on E minor pentatonic (E–G–A–B–D), followed by a restatement of the unison E lick. He ends the four-measure unaccompanied pickup with another standard E minor pentatonic blues lick.

At measure 5 of this example, the song's 12-bar form is initiated, wherein SRV presents the song's primary rhythm figure. The trick to performing this part properly relates to the upbeats indicated as X's; the left hand lightly lays across all of the strings while the right hand plays a forceful upstroke. The tricky part stems from alternating smoothly between the notes played on the downbeats—sounded with downstrokes—and the dead-string hits played on the upbeats—sounded with upstrokes. Also, on the upbeat of beat 2 in each measure, a low note is sounded along with the dead-string hit; it can seem tricky at first to fret notes on the low E or A string while muting all of the other strings with the left hand. In essence, Stevie created a rhythm guitar part that simultaneously emulates a bass line (on the downbeats) and a dead-string rhythm guitar (on the upbeats). Notice in particular his use of upstrokes when playing the two-note figure in measure 11, beats 2 and 3.

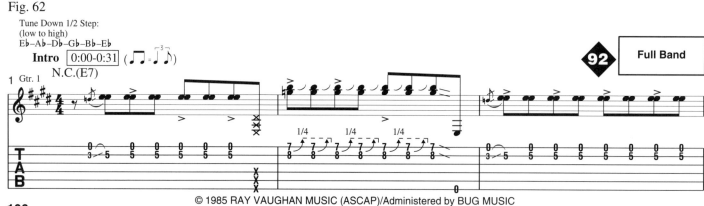

Fig. 62

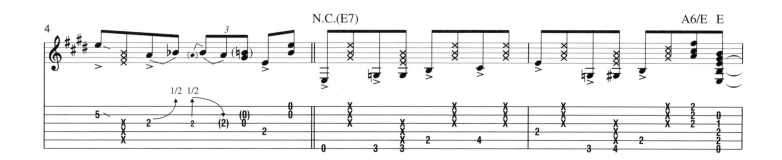

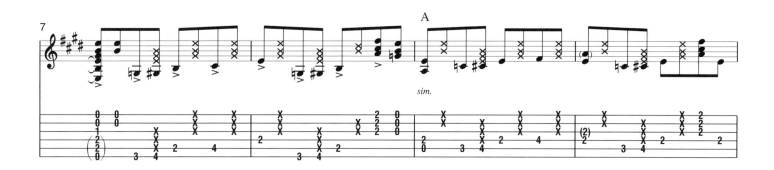

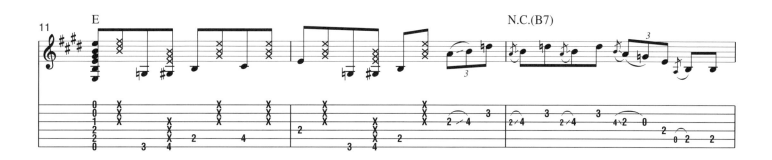

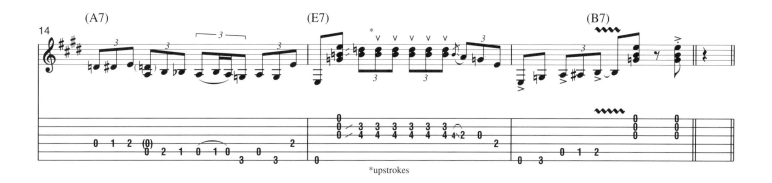

*upstrokes

Figure 63–First Verse

During the first verse, Stevie emulates the intro rhythm part by accentuating only the upbeats. Instead of playing dead-string hits, however, he usually plays the top three strings open. In measures 5 and 6, he accents an A7 chord along with the drum accents, and in measures 9–12 he basically restates what was played at this point during the intro.

Of note is the lick in measure 11, upbeat of beat 3, where he executes a "reverse rake." While fretting a B (third string) and a D (second string), he drags the pick across the top three strings, including the open high E string, moving from the high E to the fretted G string. He then quickly slides down the G string from B to A. This lick recurs several times during the song.

Fig. 63

Figure 64–Third Verse (stop chorus)

At the third verse, SRV initiates "stop" figures that are played by the entire band; he begins in the pickup measure, which is the last measure of the second verse, and in measures 2 and 3 of the "stop" chorus, the band hits hard on the downbeat of "one," followed by silence. In measure 5, he plays a figure based on E minor pentatonic which employs upstrokes, akin to the previously discussed lick in measure 11 of the intro. In measures 6 and 7, he plays a rhythm figure similar to that used during the intro, and follows in measures 7 and 8 with E minor pentatonic improvisation. He uses an alternating "high string-low string" strumming pattern for B7 in measure 10 and closes out the chorus with three measures of E minor pentatonic improvisation, utilizing many of the same licks presented earlier.

Figure 65–Solo, First Chorus

Stevie begins his solo with an Elmore James-like "Dust My Broom"/"Sweet Home Chicago" lick played on the top three strings, incorporating the open high E string. In measures 4–7, he plays straightforward E minor pentatonic lines, accentuating the eighth-note triplet feel of the song. Notice in particular the subtle half-step bends, from D to D♯, in measure 4.

In measure 8, Stevie dramatically shifts down to first position via a fast slide down the G string and continues soloing in that position, still favoring E minor pentatonic. Again, watch for the restatement of certain licks and figures that were played previously.

Fig. 65

Solo, First Chorus | 1:40-2:02 |

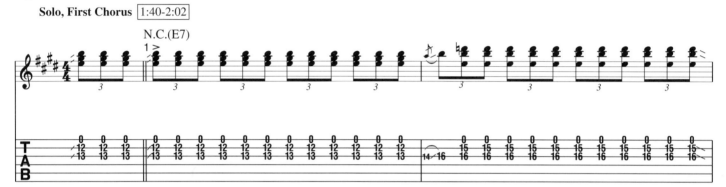

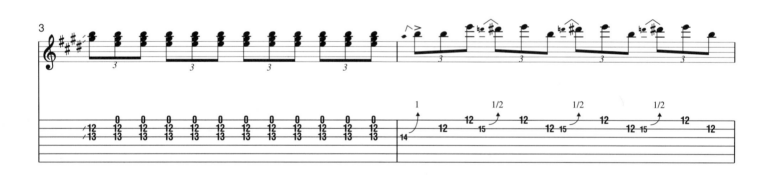

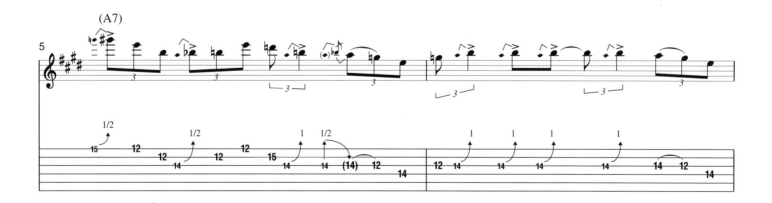

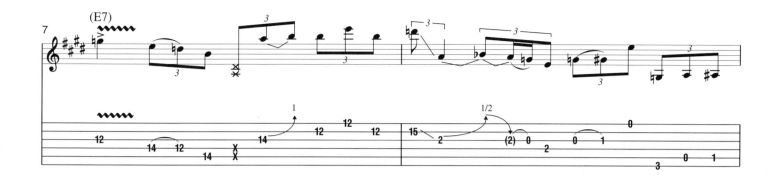

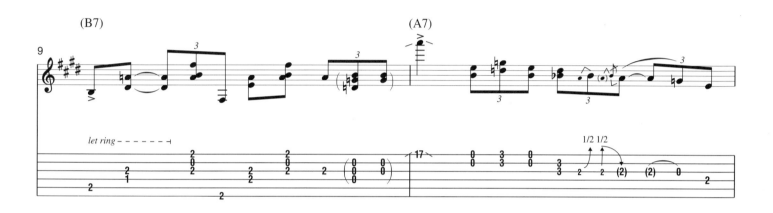

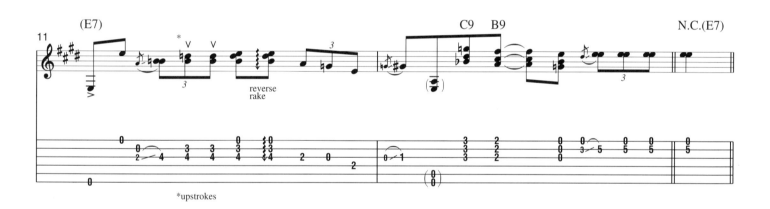

*upstrokes

Figure 66–Solo, Second Chorus

SRV begins this second chorus of improvisation with a recap of the unison E lick and "country blues" phrases stated at the very beginning of the song. In measures 5 and 6, he plays an effective lick on the top three strings over A7 that accentuates the open high E string, quickly sliding down to first position at the end of measure 6, where he remains for the rest of the solo. Once again, all of the lines are based on E minor pentatonic, and Stevie's phrases encapsulate many standard blues lines within an inspired and spontaneous performance. His massive tone stems from his penchant for using very heavy strings (.013–.058) and very large frets. Stevie also always *attacked* the guitar with great physical exertion.

Fig. 66
Solo, Second Chorus 2:03-2:26